M.V.S.C.

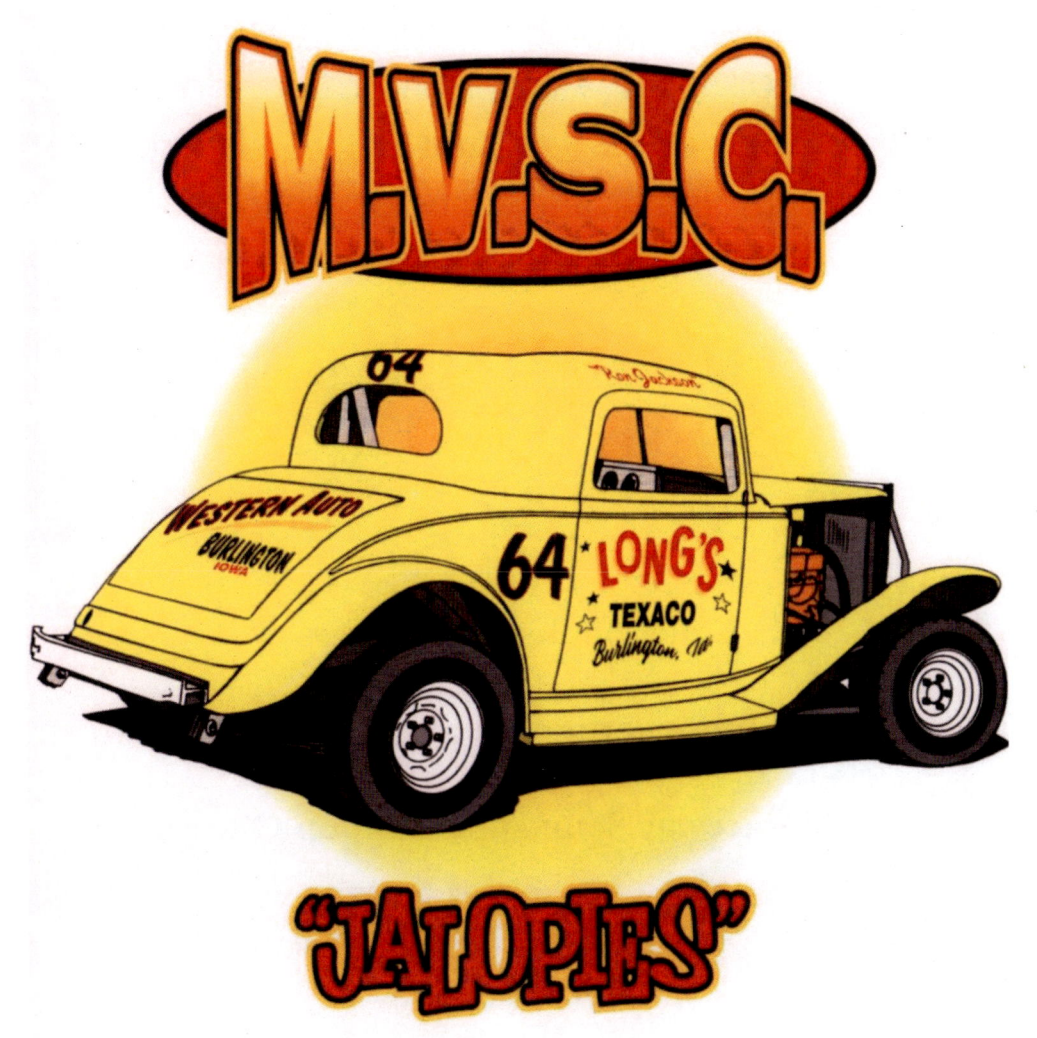

"JALOPIES"

By

Ned H Fry

© 2021 Ned H Fry

I would like to dedicate this book to Ron Jackson – racer & promoter. He wasn't superman – but I thought he came close. I would like to also thank the Jackson family for allowing me to conduct his funeral. It was an honor.

Other books by Ned Fry

Monkey Ranch Engineering: Tarantula Flats, New Mexico

34 Raceway Semi supers Group One

If I wouldn't have raced my whole life, I would be richer & had less pain, but today I would do it all over again. What a ride.

Ned H Fry

JALOPY RACING

by Gene Jackson

The Mississippi Valley Speedway Club, which became known simply as MVSC was organized in 1956. The original president/promoter of the Club was Ray Scarff of Trenton, Iowa. The club was interested in racing what they called jalopies and issued memberships to ninety nine individuals that wanted to participate in dirt track racing. Memberships were limited to ninety nine because the membership number was also the number placed on the car and they didn't want three digit numbers on the race cars. If you wanted to join the club and participate in the racing you could only obtain a membership by buying one of the original memberships from a member that no longer raced. Mr. Scarff was able to make arrangements with three southeast Iowa county fairboards to conduct a jalopy racing program. at Columbus Jct, Mt. Pleasant and West Liberty on a perodic basis. All three county fairboards had a one-half mile horse racing facility that could be converted to auto racing. Each weekend from April into September a race was to be held at one of the three fairground facilities. Allen Samberg of Burlington, Iowa assumed the position of president/promoter of the club in 1960 and he made arrangements with Lee and Des Moines county fairboards to conduct an occasional race in Donnellson and Burlington. The club was to share a percentage of the gate receipts with each fairboard and that money was used to pay the racing officials, the racing insurance premiums and prize money to drivers for participating in the racing program. The club conducted jalopy races on a weekly basis from 1956 through 1965. Earl Reynolds officiated MVSC races for many years and one of his many memories of the early years was conducting time trials with a hand held stop watch.

The membership of the club agreed to a set of race car construction rules. Any American made car built from 1932 through 1948 could be raced. The vehicle raced could use any factory production part that was built for that particular car from the years 1932 through 1948. For example, a 1937 Ford could use gears, transmission, engine or any other part that was factory produced for any Ford car built through the years 1932 through 1948. Many participants would use a early model vehicle frame and body and install later produced engines and transmissions. The early frame and body was advantageous because of lighter weight and the later model engines, brakes, transmissions etc. provided more efficiency and power. No racing parts were allowed, only factory production parts could be used. Engines could be bored to sixty thousands over stock, but no more. Anyone suspected of using illegal parts could be protested by any other competitor for a $25 "tear down" fee and the parts would be examined by club officials. The penalty for use of illegal parts was disqualification from any future racing. A friend of mine, Dale Murray, has told me that the first year the jalopies were raced he remembers there was no roll cage or even a roll bar in at least one of the cars. Of course as the competition evolved into more competative racing all cars were required to have roll cages and safety belts. MVSC has always been proud of the fact that in nearly ten years of racing they never had a fatality. Over the years there were two scary injuries, neither of which were life threatening.

The weekly racing program consisted of seven events. There were time trials, a five lap trophy dash, four ten lap heat races, a twelve lap semi main and a twenty lap feature event. The feature event had a unique starting lineup arrangement in that the fast cars started near the rear of the field. The race started twenty cars made up of the four top finishers from each heat and the top four from the semi main. The sixteen cars qualified for the feature from the heat races were lined up with the car that had the slowest time from the time trials starting inside on the front row and the car with the fastest time from the time trials starting outside of row eight. The first few years the semi main qualifiers were placed at the front of the feature. Drivers learned to take advantage of dropping out of heat races and qualifying for the feature through the semi main so as to start in the front of the feature. That lineup rule was changed and those qualifiers were there after placed in rows nine and ten of the feature event. The race fans loved the start of those feature races as drivers with fast cars would make some dare devil moves trying to beat everyone else to the front of the pack.

MVSC jalopy racing developed a large spectator following. Many of the drivers became crowd favorites or in a few cases a driver might be considered a villain if he should out run one of the fan favorites. I am aware of one racing event in Columbus Jct where fans had to be turned away an hour before race time because the grandstand was already full with no more seating available. The vehicles that showed up as race cars were usually not cars taken off the street but were probably recovered from a junk yard or rescued from behind a barn somewhere. The cars were unprofessionally prepared machines that most likely were built in a back yard shed or the family garage. The pit crews were a collection of family members and friends of the driver that had probably helped build the car. A majority of the fellows that drove those colorful old vintage machines have now passed away. The pictures in this book and some sixty year old memories are all that is left of those loveable old jalopies and the drivers that once thrilled the race fans in packed grandstands as they raced each other around the half mile dirt tracks in southeast Iowa so many years ago.

Author's note: Much of the information contained in this article was provided by Earl Reynolds of Mt.Pleasant, Iowa and Dale Murray of West Burlington, Iowa

My Hero Lived Down the Street

When I was about 7 years old, my mother finally let me ride my bike around town. My first discovery was a race shop just down the street. It had a sign above the door saying, Wayne Lee Racing #89. Beside the garage was a pile of old racecar parts, bent up fenders, doors and blown up engines. No one was around and I made a mental note to come back later to check it out. I then went to explore the rest of the town.

Days later I rode by and there was a group of men working on a racecar. I stopped but stayed at a distance. They talked, worked and then talked some more. They noticed me but made no comment. Days later I returned and the same people were working again. This time I was a little braver so I rode up on my bike. I asked what they were doing. One of the men said (getting her ready for Saturday night.) I asked why they called the car her. They all laughed and said it's fickle like a woman. I laughed too, but didn't understand. I watched, but never got off my bike and after awhile I went home.

Monday afternoon I returned and found the car wrecked, sitting on a trailer. No one was around, so I climbed up on the trailer to look inside. I was amazed it had only one seat and a single roll bar behind the seat, two gauges, no carpet or radio. It was nothing like my Dad's car. The roof and hood were all caved in. I returned later to find the men taking it off the trailer. I wanted to help but was told to stay back. Once they got it on the ground, they let me help push it into the garage. I wasn't much help, but I thought I was big stuff. The radiator was crushed in and was replaced. Once that was done, they started that stand around and talk business again. I wanted to see them start it and hear it run. They finally got around to starting the thing. It was a V8 Ford flat head with stubby headers. WOW that was loud!! I couldn't wait to tell my Mom about how loud it was and all she said was, THAT'S NICE. Not the answer I expected; the word nice and racecar did not seem to go together.

That's pretty much how the summer went. Fridays, watch them work and Monday, stop to see how they did. The driver's name was Wayne Lee. The car was a 1940 Ford Coupe. It was painted white and black with full fenders, trimmed for the tires. The lettering was red trimmed in black. It had several names of taverns and a gas station painted on the sides. It had a big 89 on each side and the roof. Above each door was the name Wayne Lee in red script. I learned my first race car lesson that day. Wayne told me that you should always spend the extra money to have a professional painter letter your car. The sponsor wants it to look good for their money. He said there was nothing worse than a home- made lettering job. I always asked a lot of questions. They always laughed but never failed to give me an answer.

The following summer started just like the prior, except I discovered the people across the street went to all the races. One Saturday I just went over and stood by their car until they came out and I asked to go along. I had to get my mom's approval and we were off. I watched my hero set fast time, win the heat and he finished second in the feature. Monday, I had a whole list of new questions for Wayne. The rest of the summer I never had to ask if I could go along, I just showed up at the right time and we went. That was my first full summer of racing. I watched them work on the car, then saw the results on Saturday. Sadly, that ended up being my hero's last year of racing.

Twenty some years later, I sat in my sprint car, waiting to be pushed off for hot laps on a terrible racetrack. An old man with a walker came up to my car and leaned into the cockpit. He told me to take it easy, that the track was in no shape to run fast yet. It was Wayne Lee, my childhood hero. I could not believe it!!! I had only seen him once or twice since I was small. I thanked him and told him how glad I was to see him. Then I was pushed off. When I got back, he was nowhere around. I never saw him again. I later found out that he had been very sick and had died shortly after that sprint car show.

I never forgot the time he took to answer my questions and not treat me like a little kid (which I was). He taught me to take pride in being a professional, that it's a lot of work to keep a car looking good and that little kids see and hear every thing So the next time a child asks you a question, take the time to treat them special. They will always remember it and you'll be a better person for it.

64
Ron Jackson
BURLINGTON
IOWA
64
LONG'S
TEXACO
Burlington, Ia.

SPECKS'S 66
95

8

BURLINGTON
MURRAY'S
Cities Service

97
chardson's Auto
Salvage
Phone
97
2-1968
Burlington,
Ia.

MVSC
1969
CHAMPION
SUPER
STOCKS
MVSC
1969
CHAMPION
SUPER
STOCKS
MVSC
1969
CHAMPIO
SUPER
STOCKS

M.V.S.C.
SANCTIONED
RACES
3

Darrell Kratt's first race, 1966, Columbus Jct. track

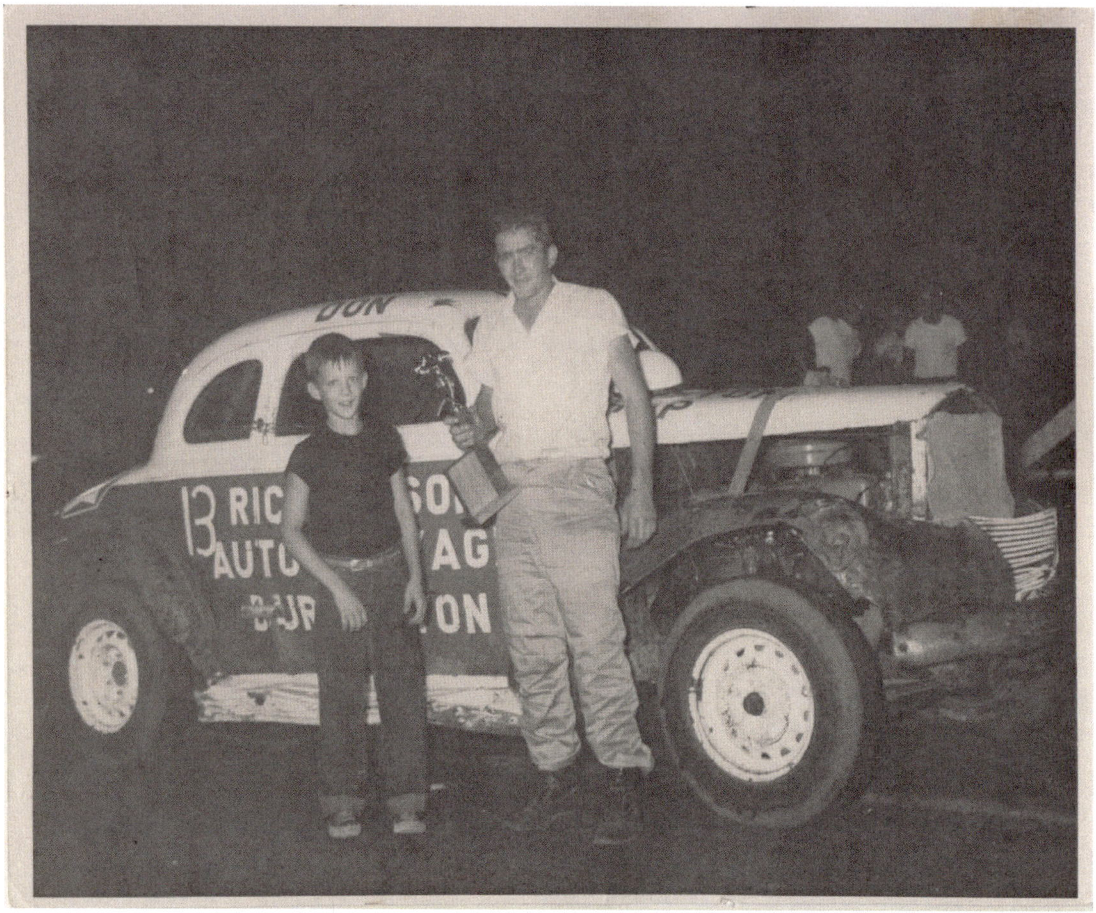
DON
13

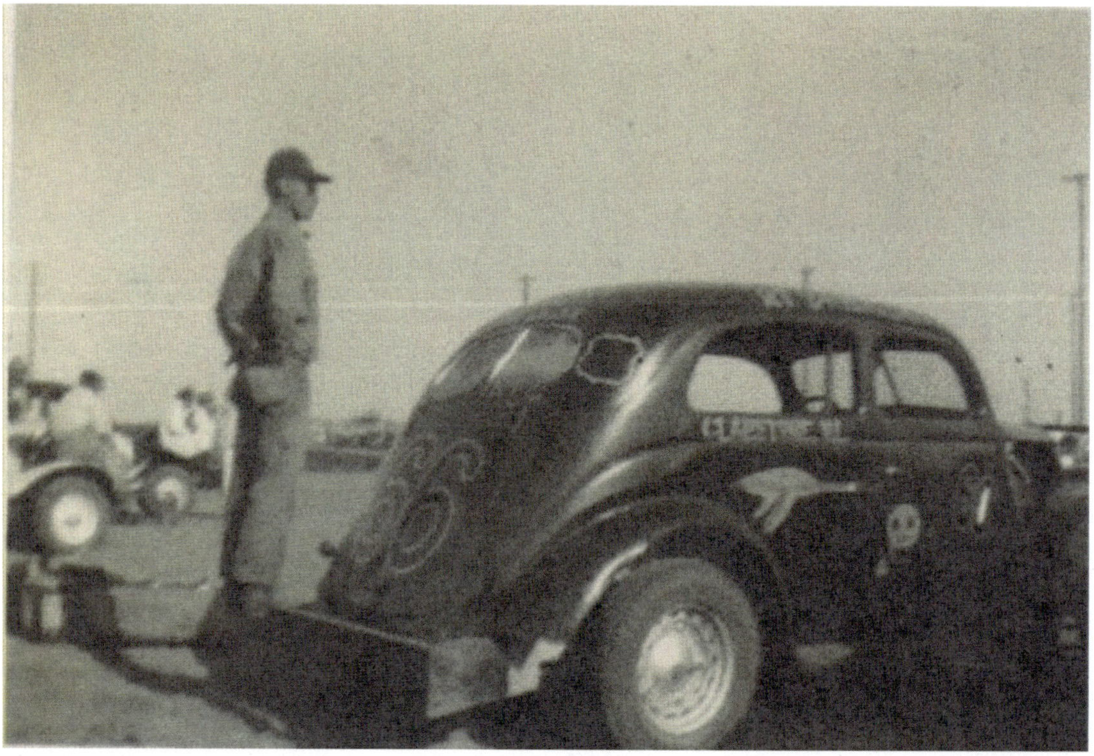

13

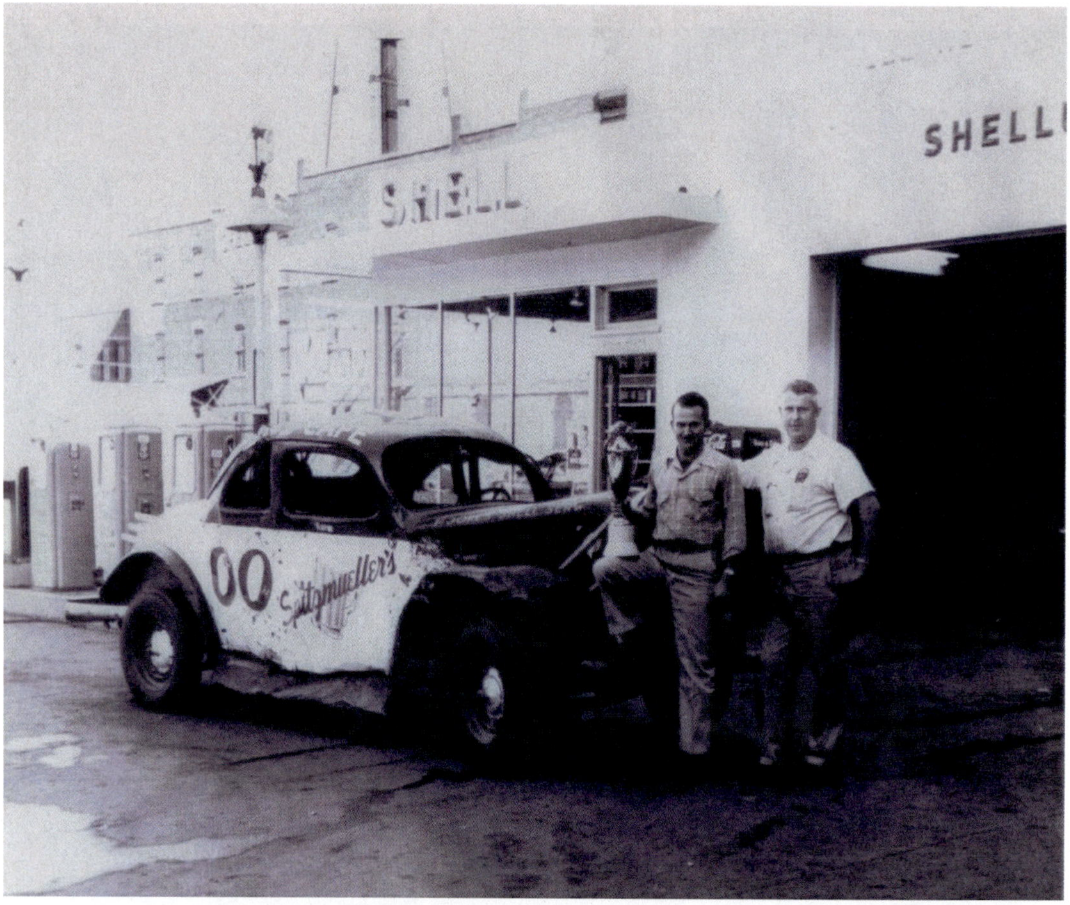
SHELL
SHELL
00
Spitzmueller's

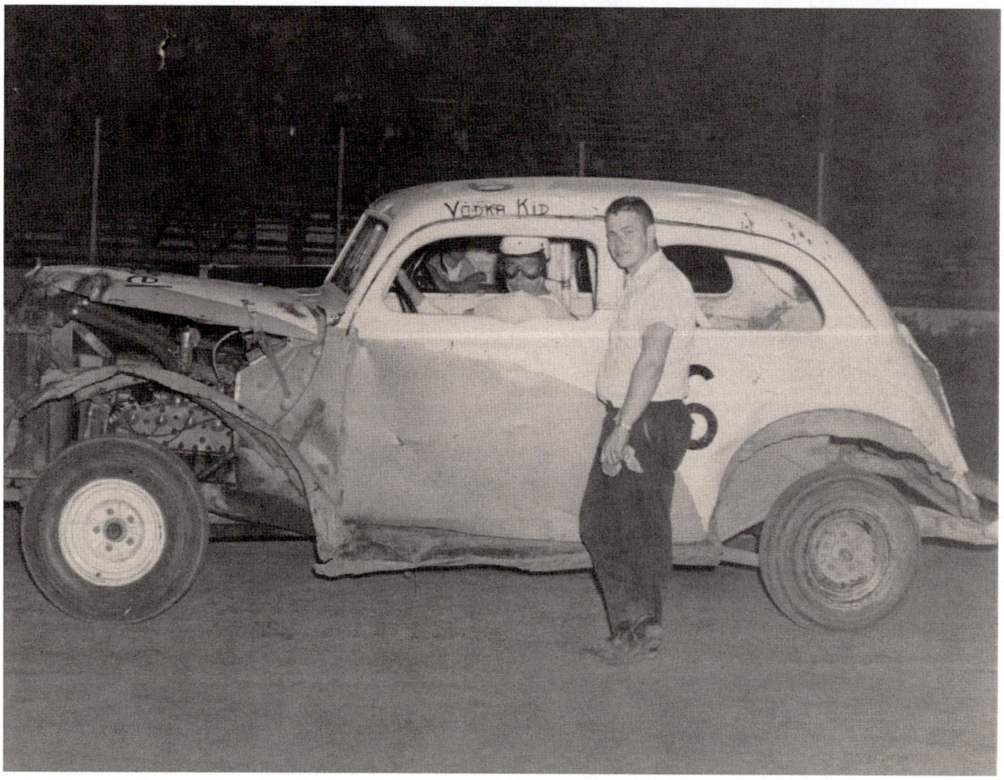
VODKA KID

Bob Ensminger

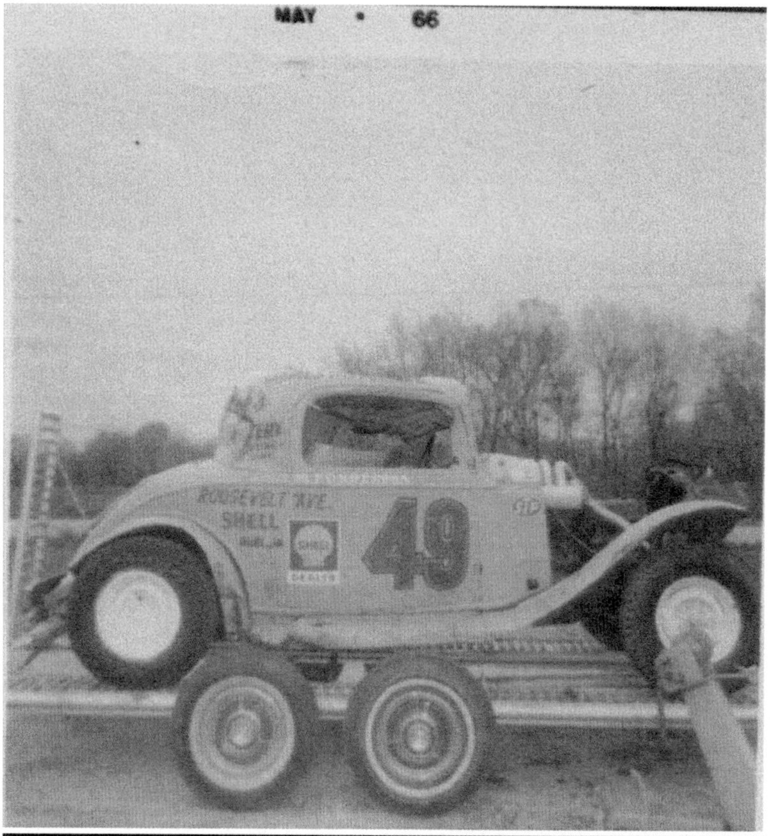
MAY • 66
ROOSEVELT AVE
SHELL
49
STP

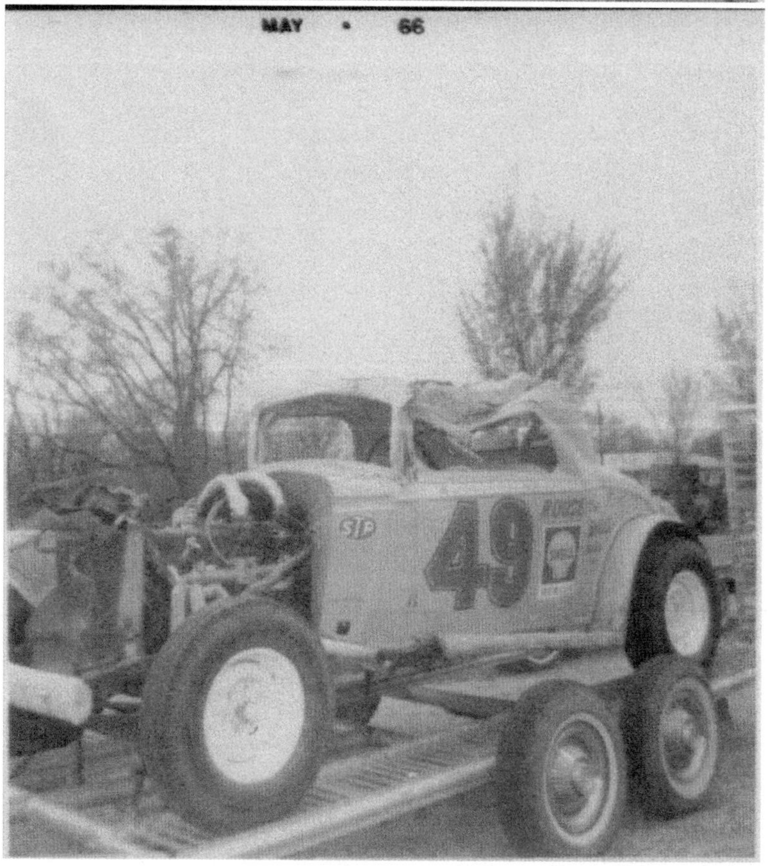
MAY • 66
STP
49

17

18

5
BURLINGTON IOWA
WHITEY'S-SINCLAIR-SERVICE
OAK-OSBORN
BURLINGTON IOWA

ECIAL
00
15
11

Bill & Scott Newman

20

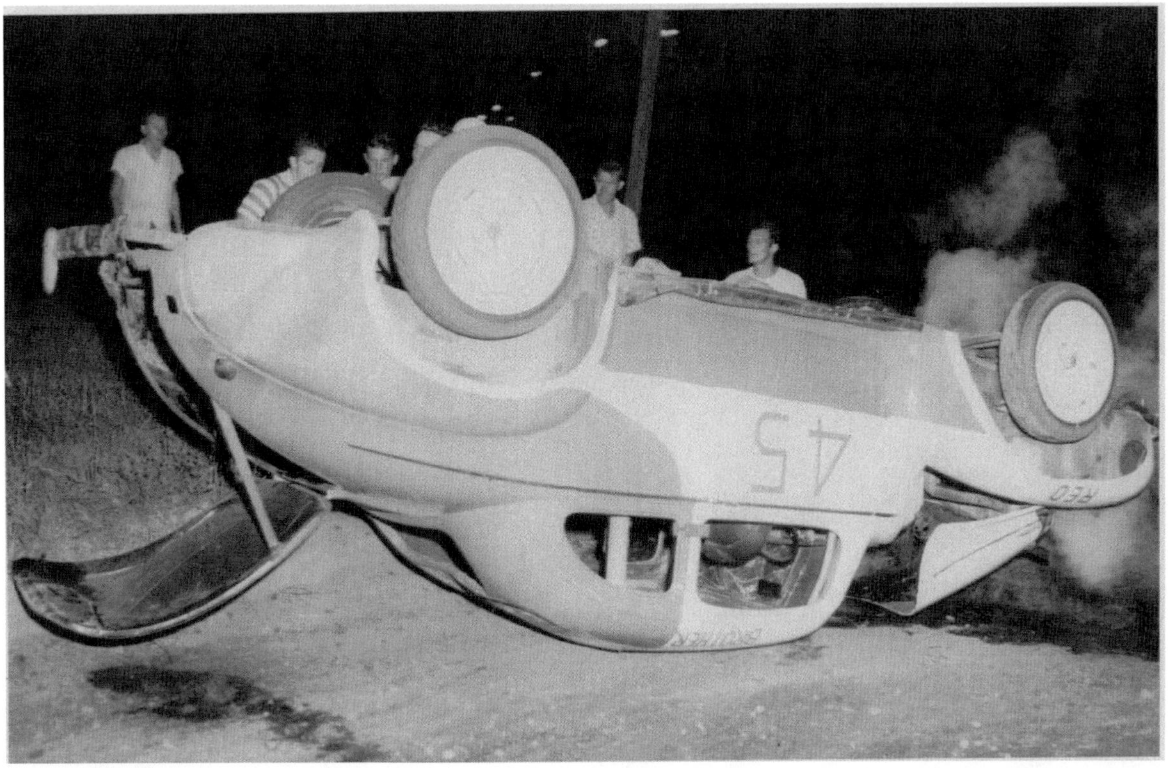
45

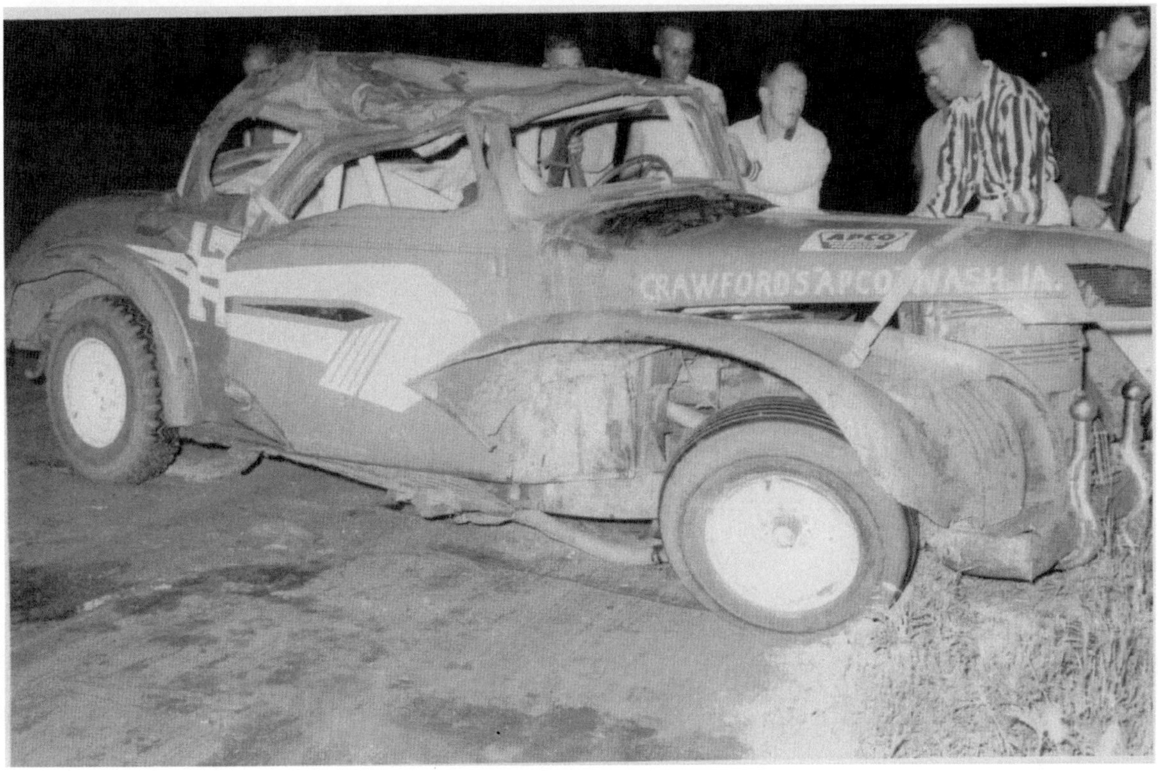
APCO

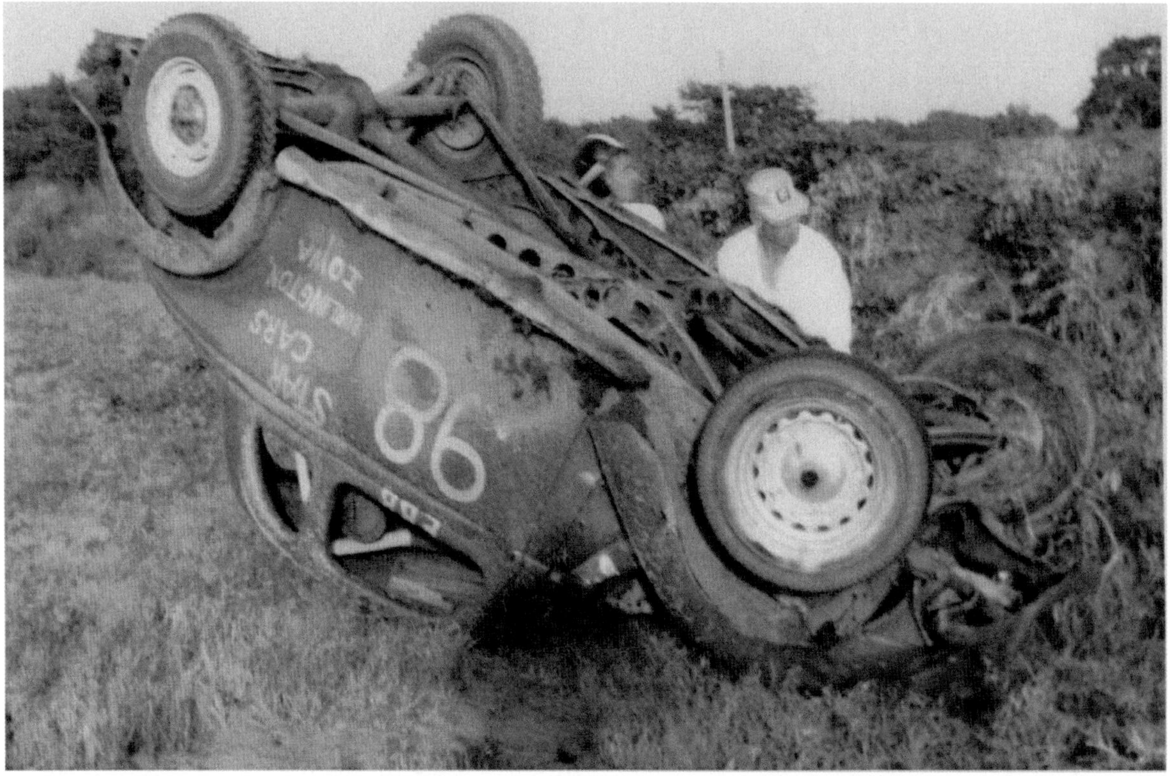

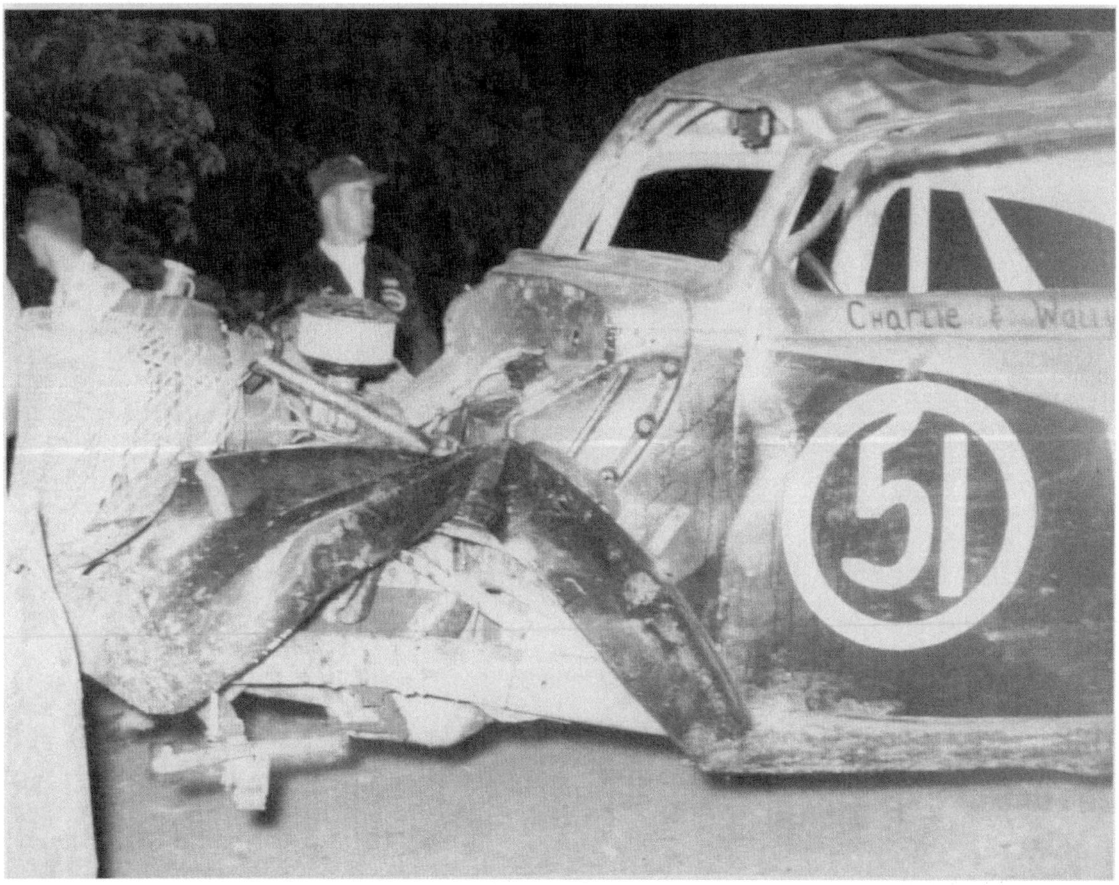
51

23

24

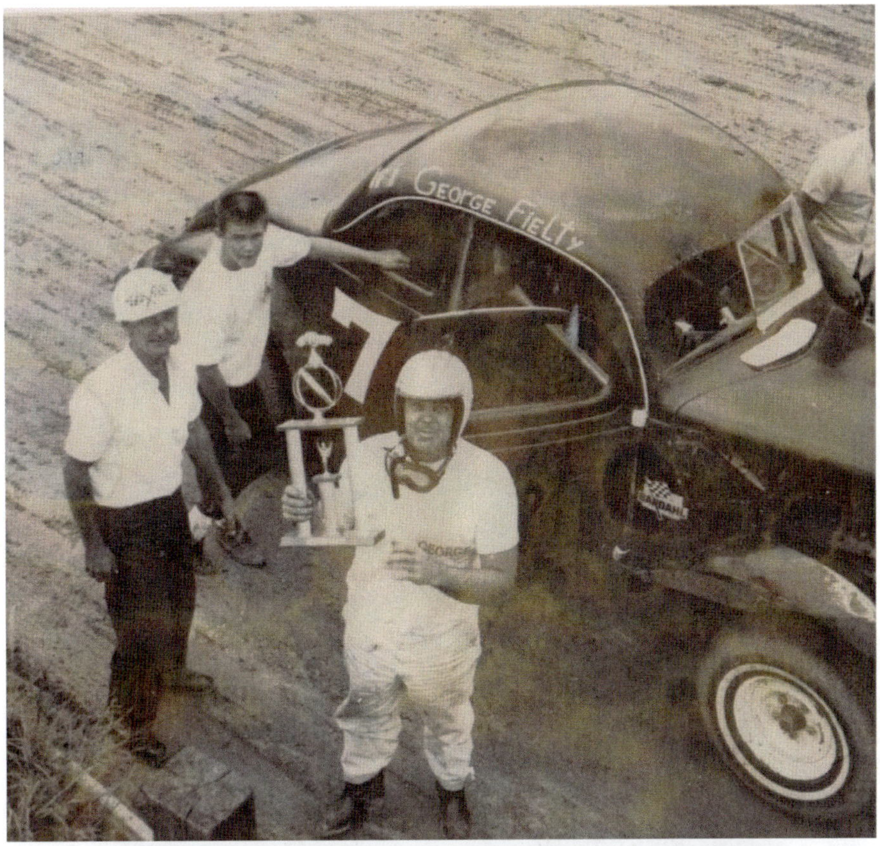
George Fielty
7

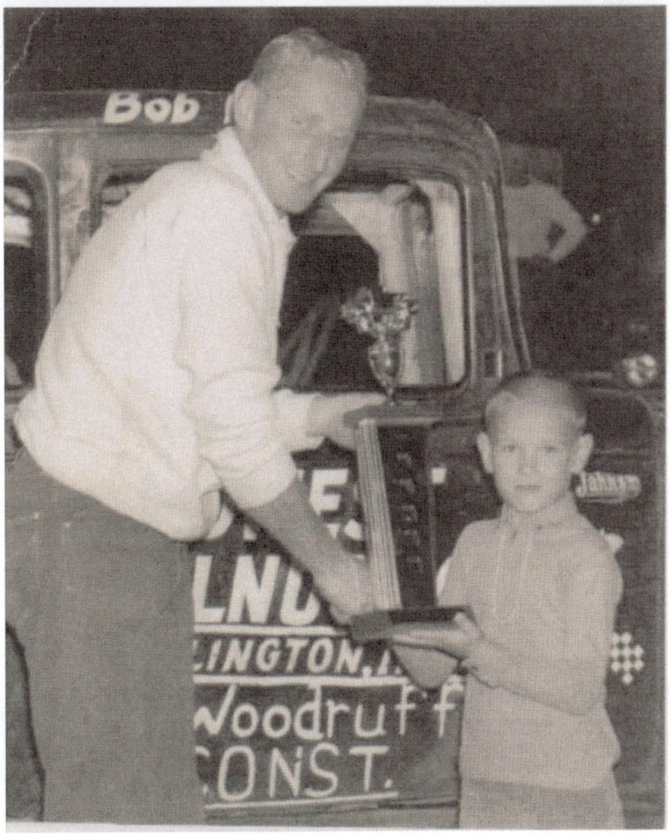
Bob
Woodruff
CONST.

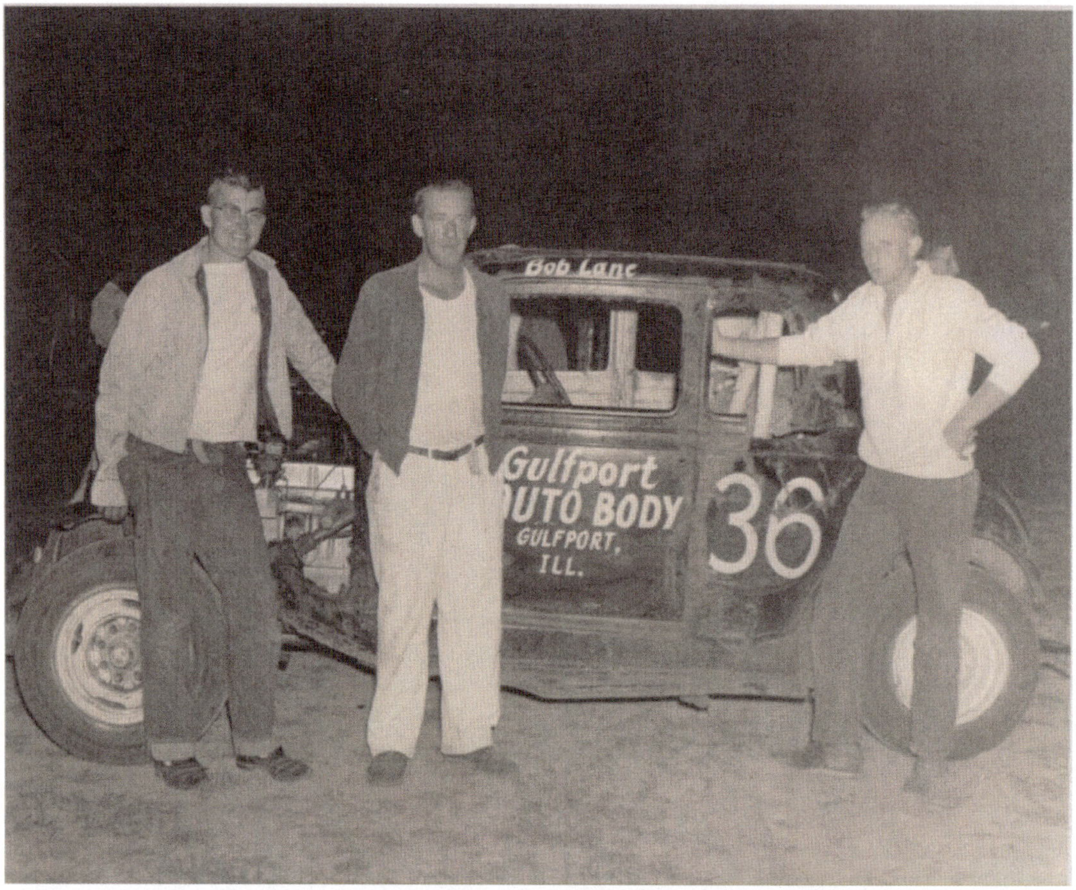
Bob Lane
Gulfport
UTO BODY
GULFPORT,
ILL.
36

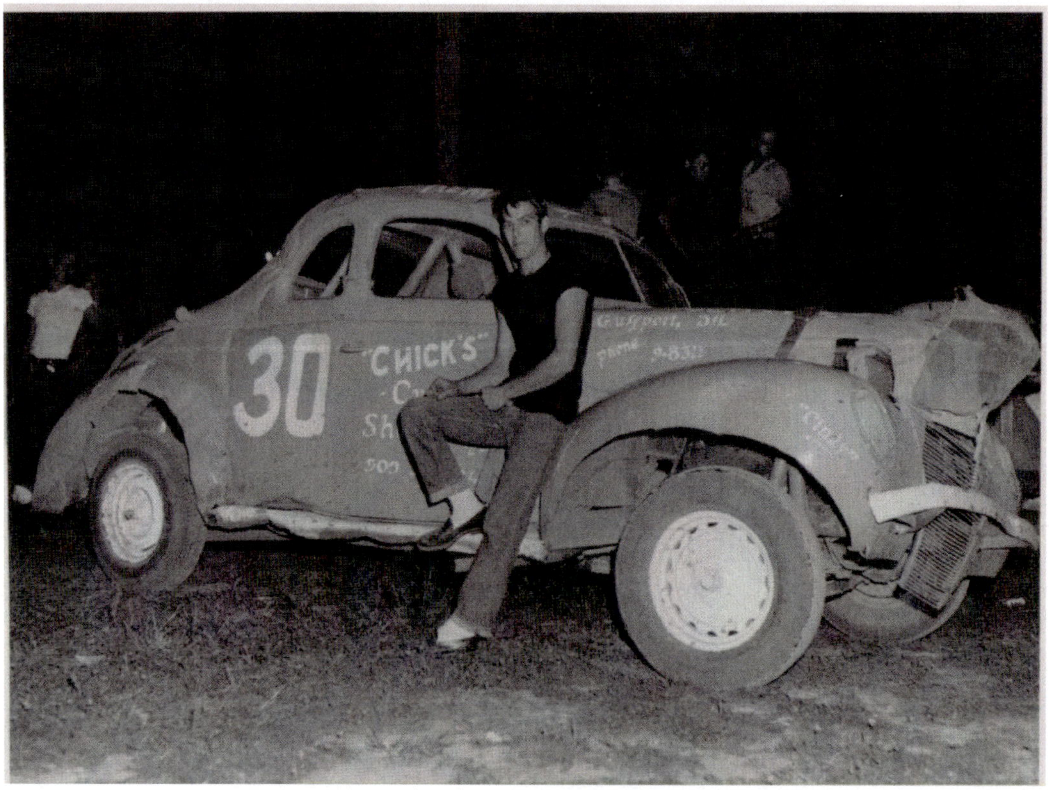
30
"CHICK'S"

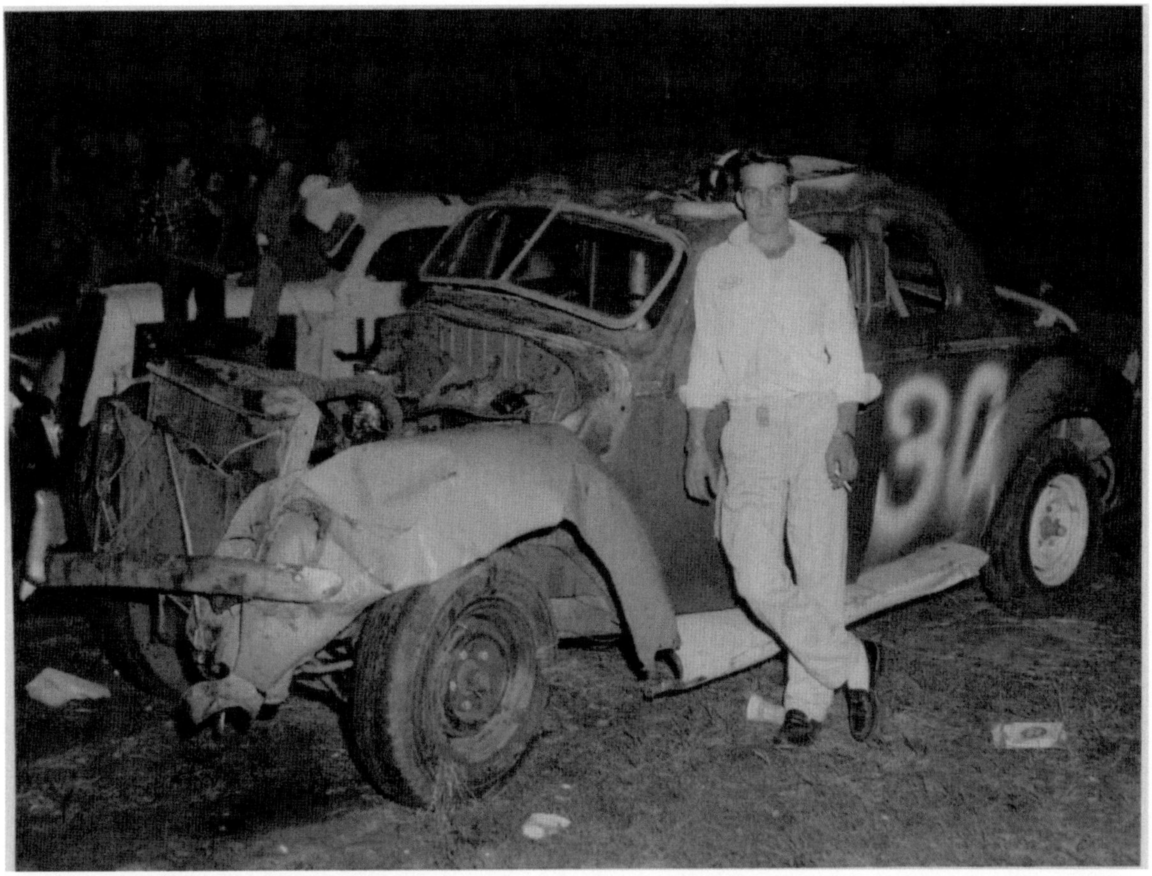
30

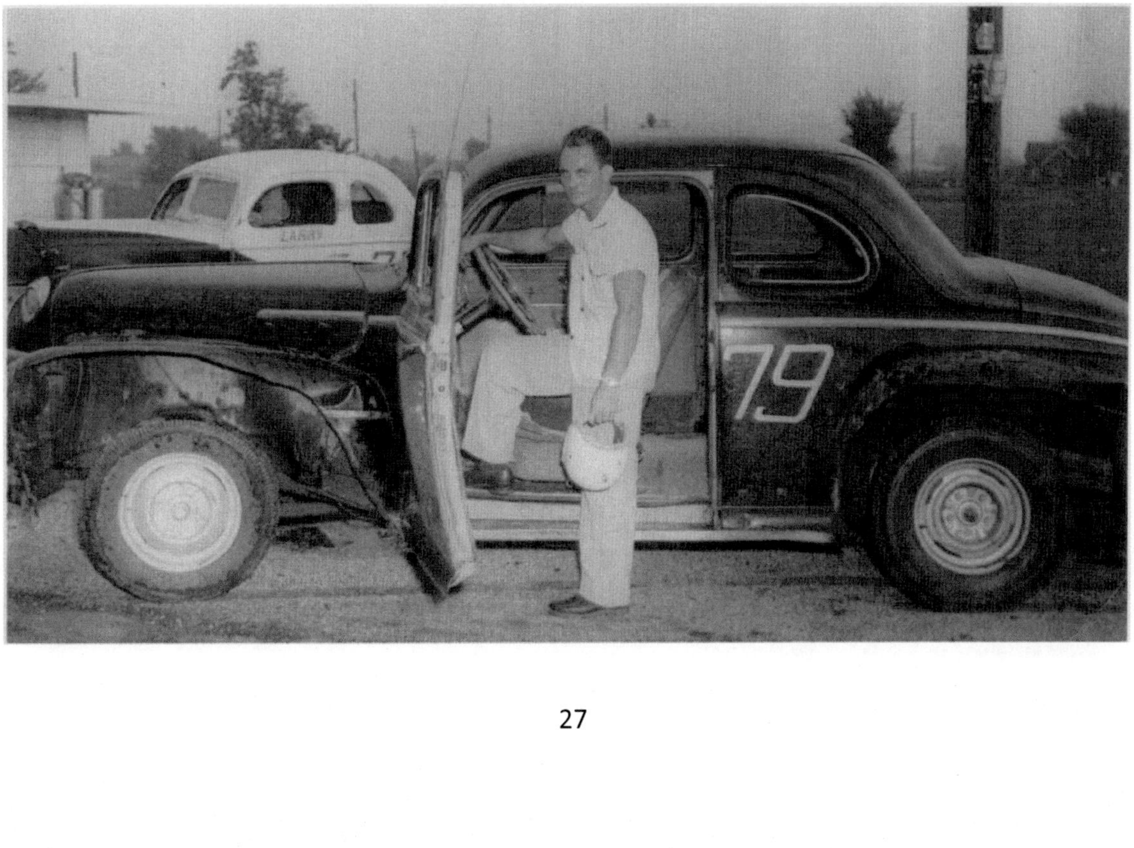
79

SANCTIONED
RACES
DALE
81
Standard
24 HR.

Bill Newman
BILL Newman
00

Wayne Noble-Wapello, IA-May, 20, 1961- Mt. Pleasant, IA.

Bill Arnold

29

Ron Jackson   April, 1961

Bob Ensminger

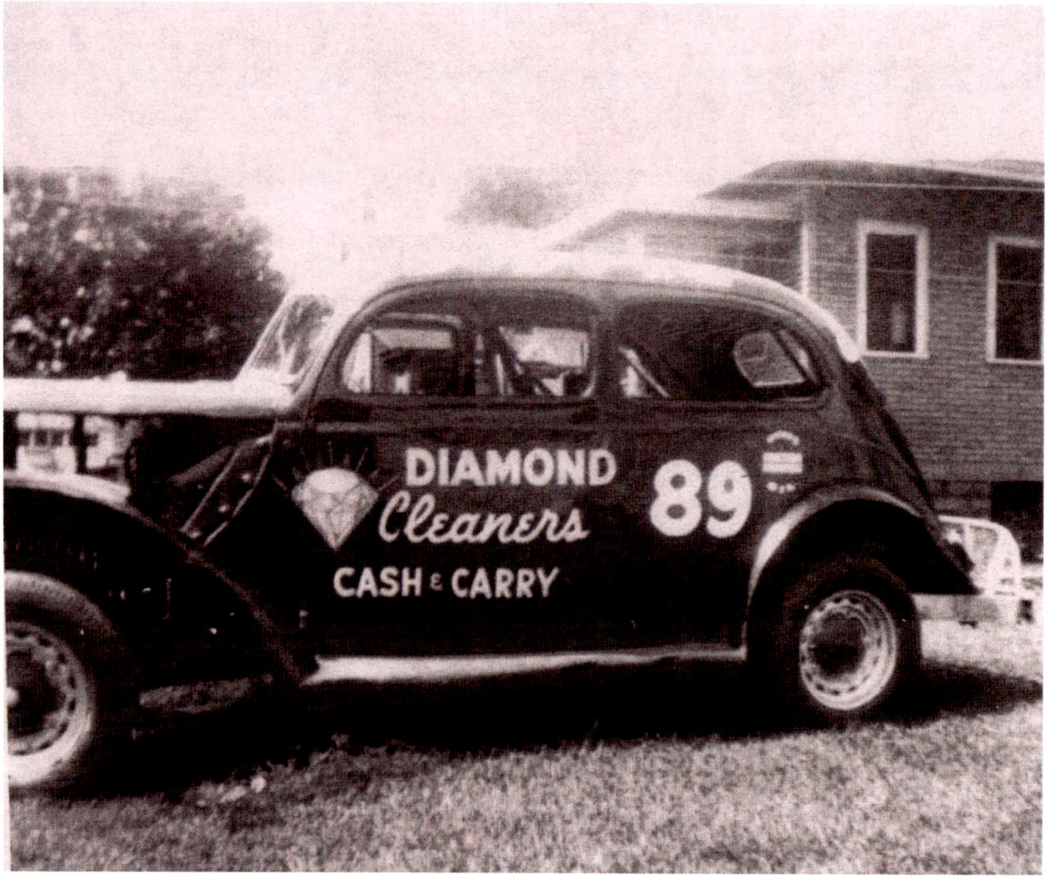
DIAMOND
Cleaners
89
CASH & CARRY

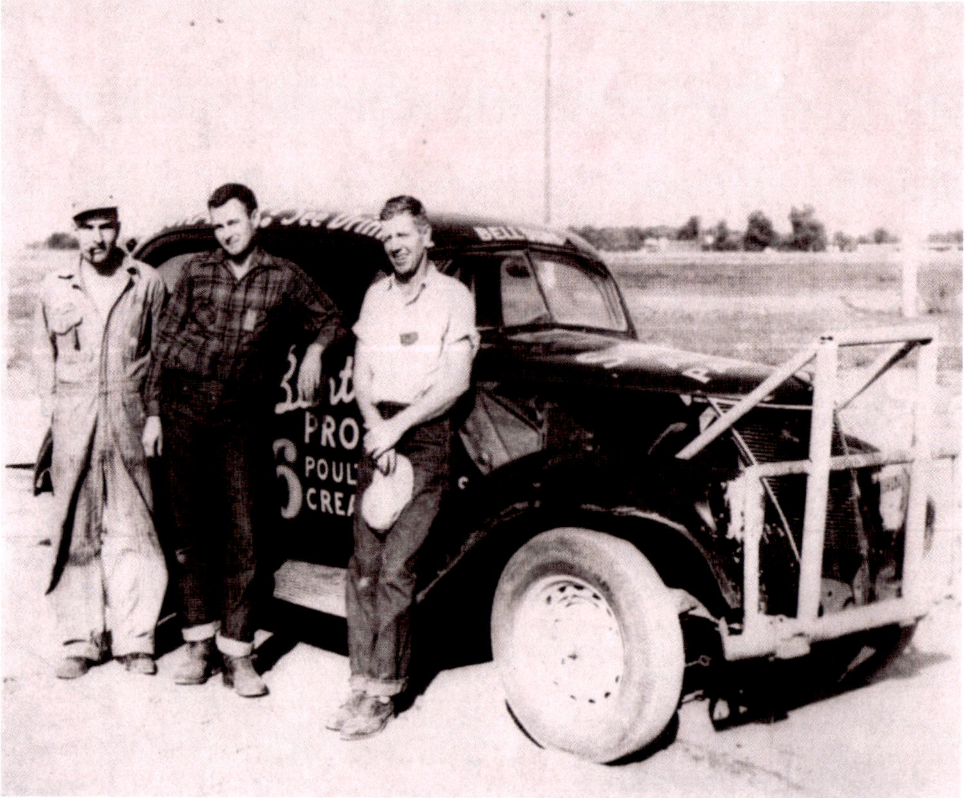

M.V.S.C.
SANCTIONED
BURLINGTON IOWA
OAK-OSBORN
BURLINGTON IOWA

41

34

Andy Anderson

ilber Heage 1961, West Liberty track

Ron Jackson

Ron Jackson's cars

1964

1962

37

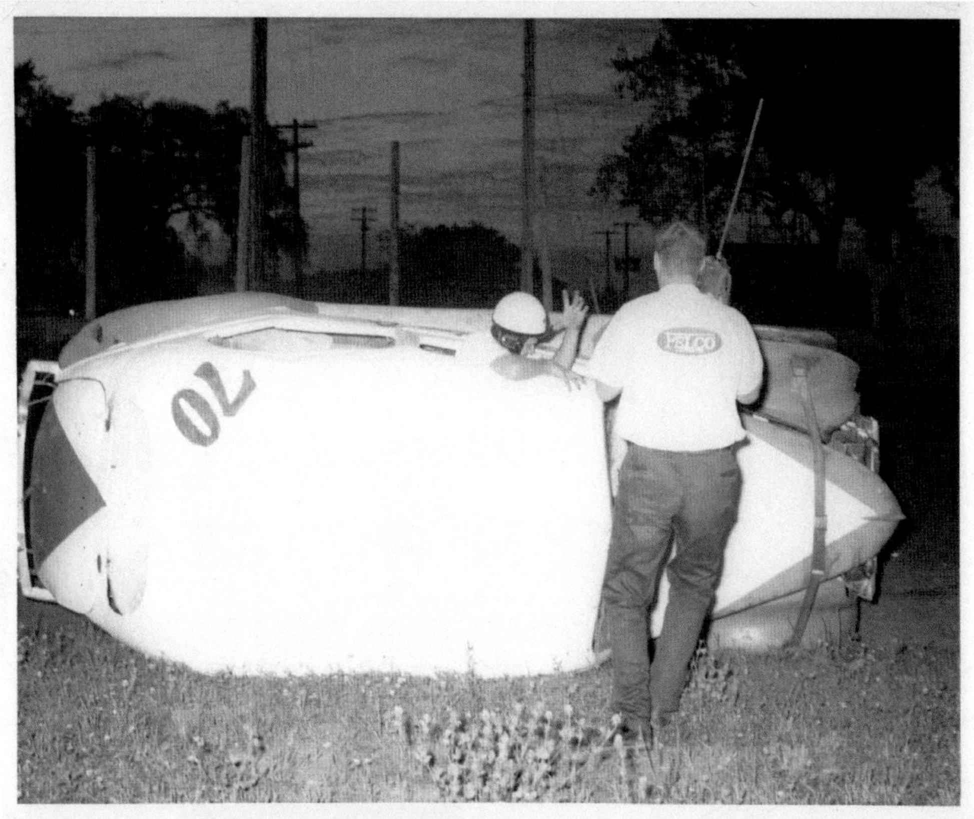

70
PELCO

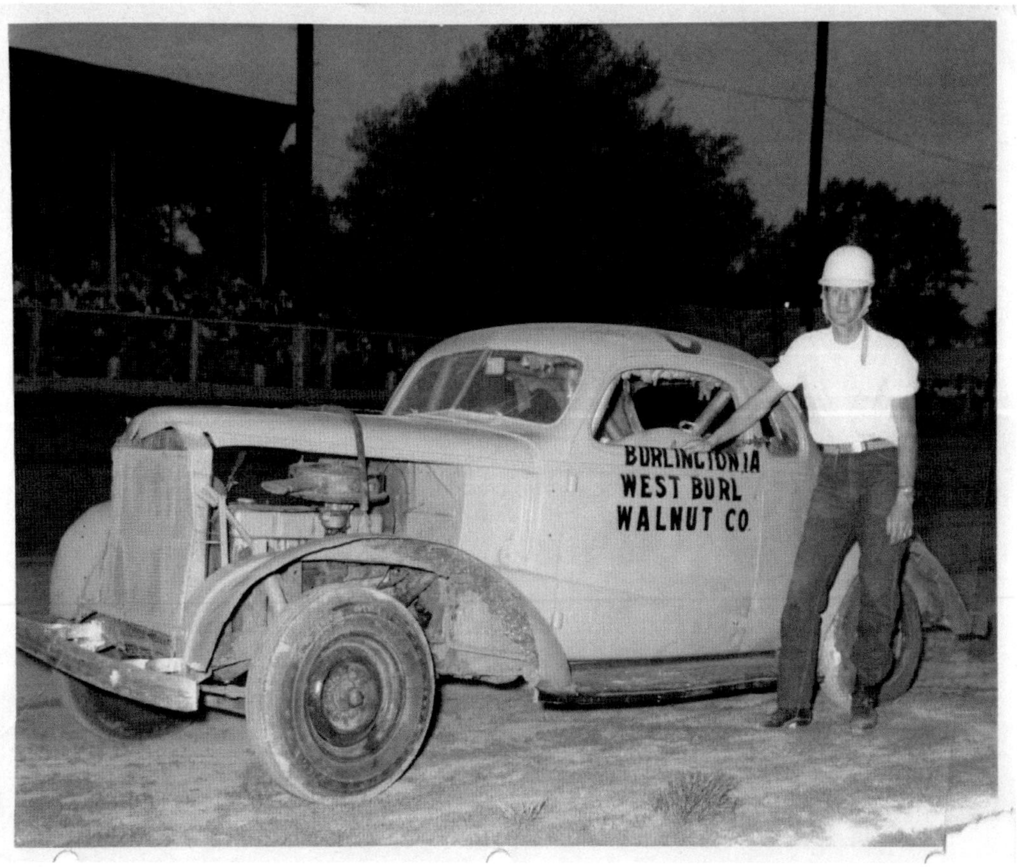

WEST BURL
WALNUT CO.

39

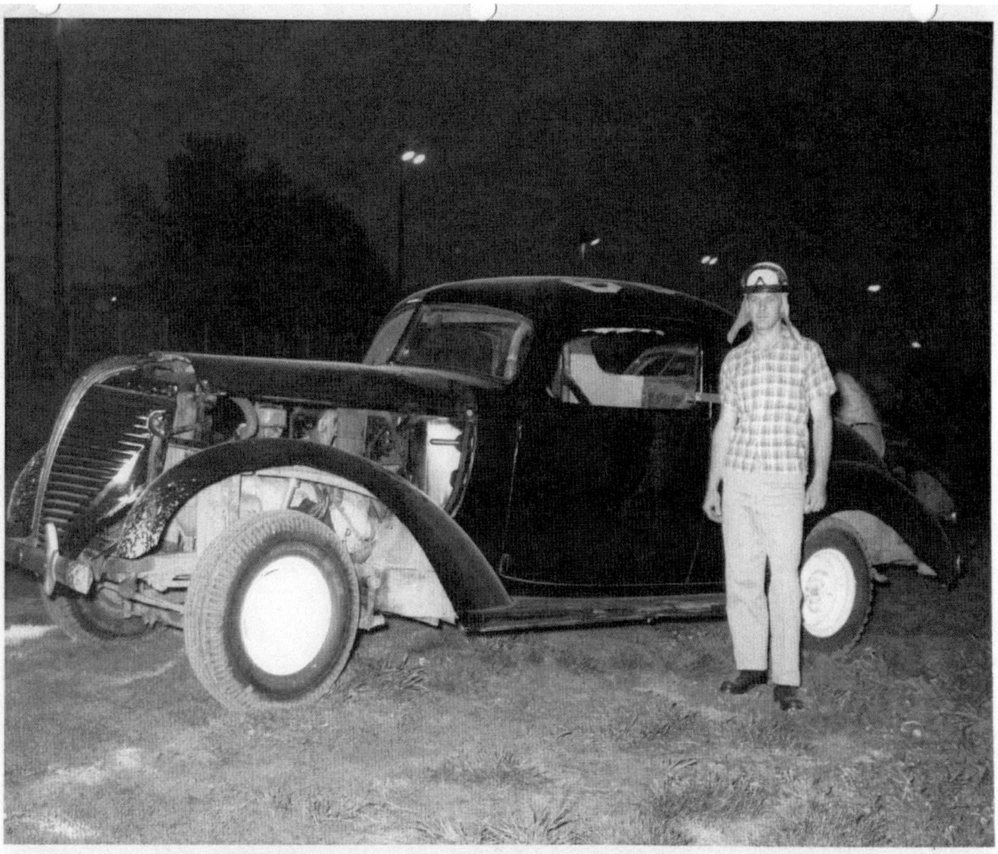

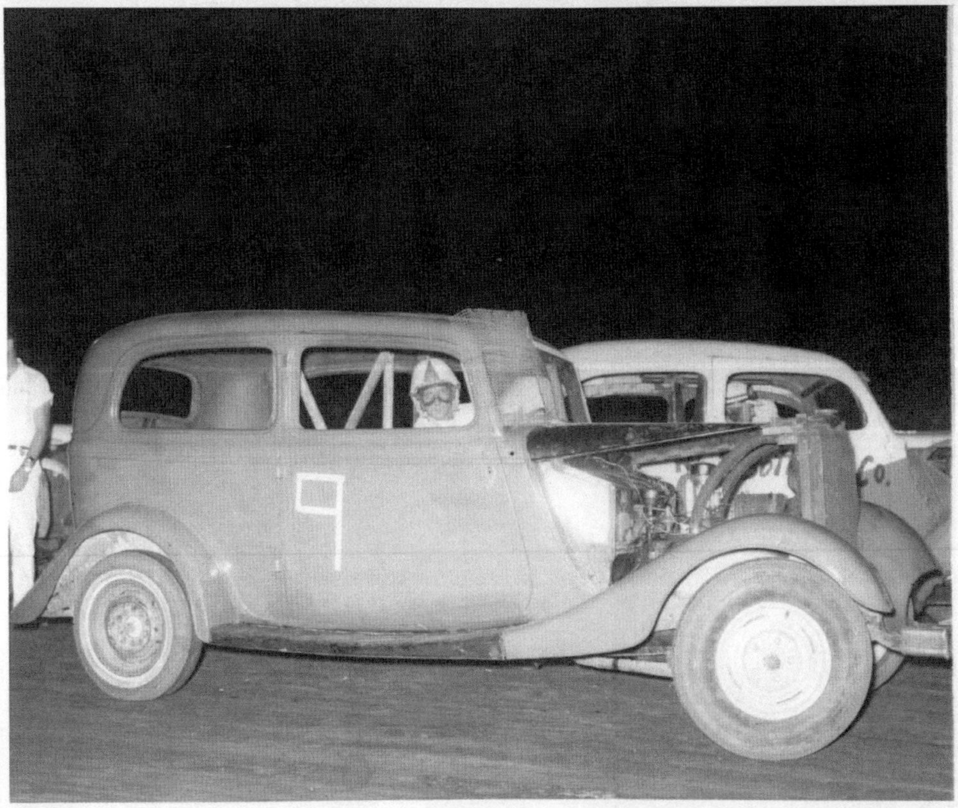
9
Co.

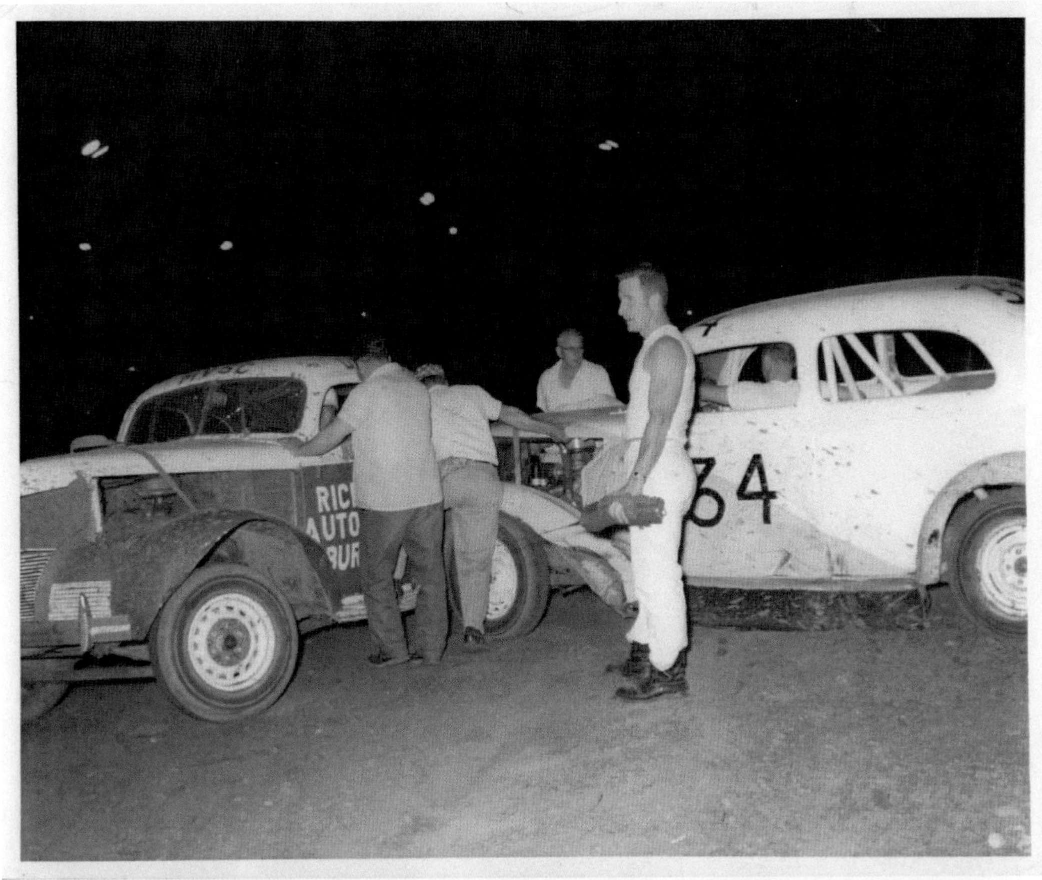
64

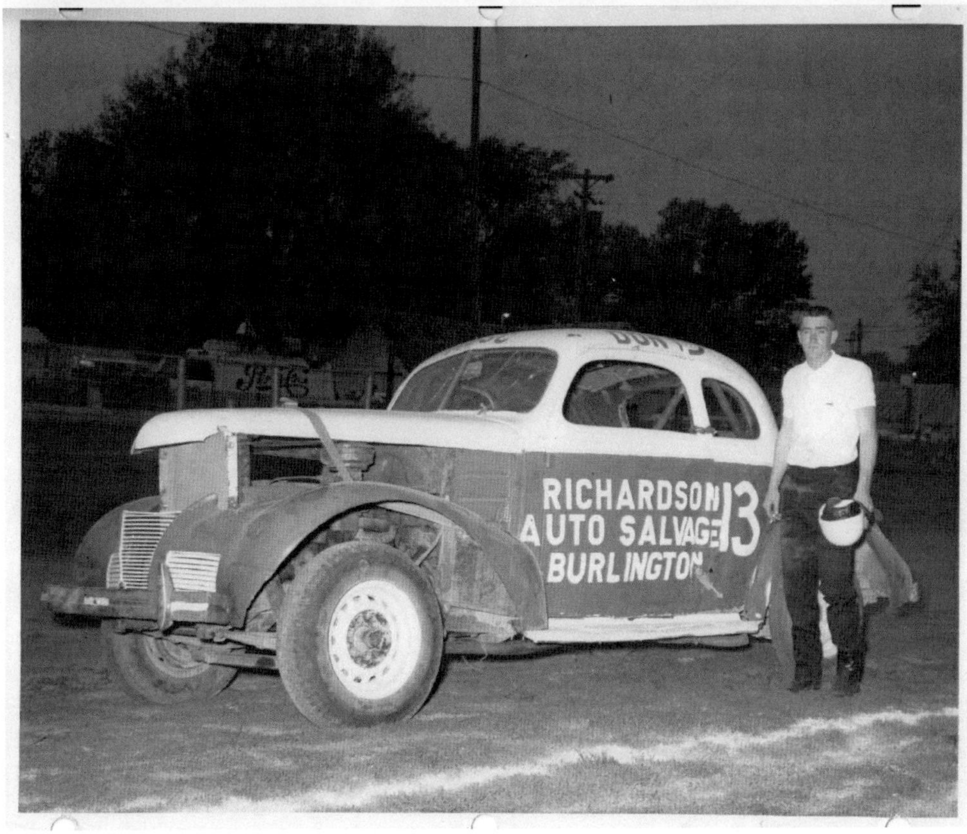
RICHARDSON
AUTO SALVAGE
BURLINGTON
13

42

M.V.S.C
SANCTIONED
RACES
Rocky's
WELDING-SALVAGE
MILTON ROCKWELL
Phone MA-7-2461
WEST
LIBERTY
IOWA
RICH
39

44

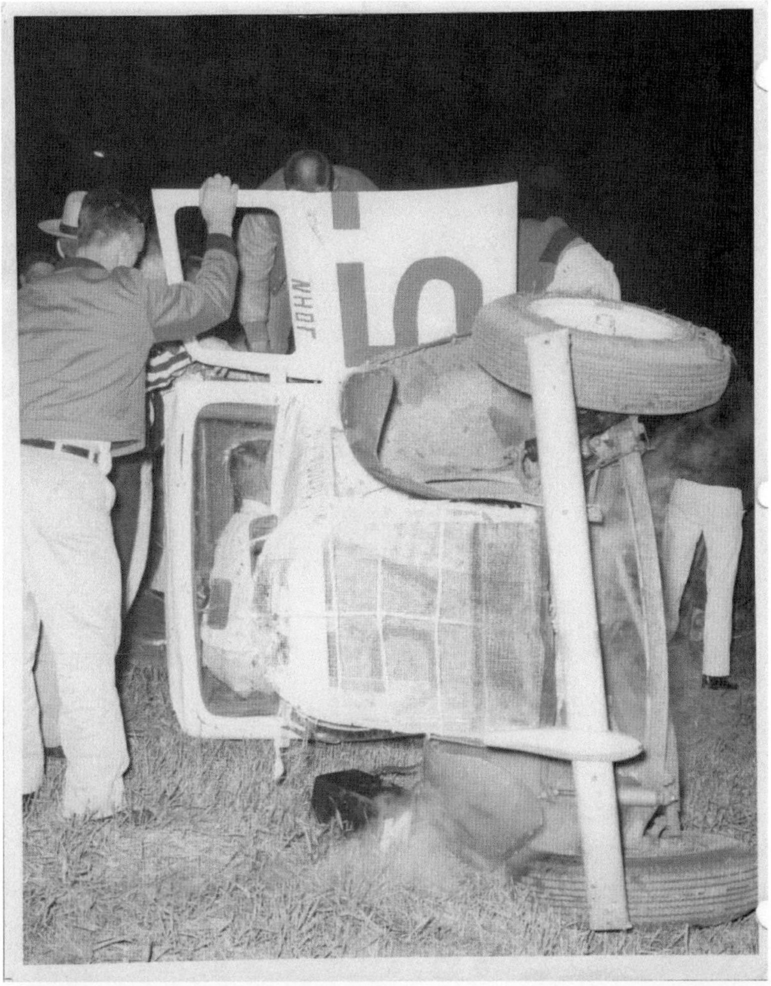
JOHN

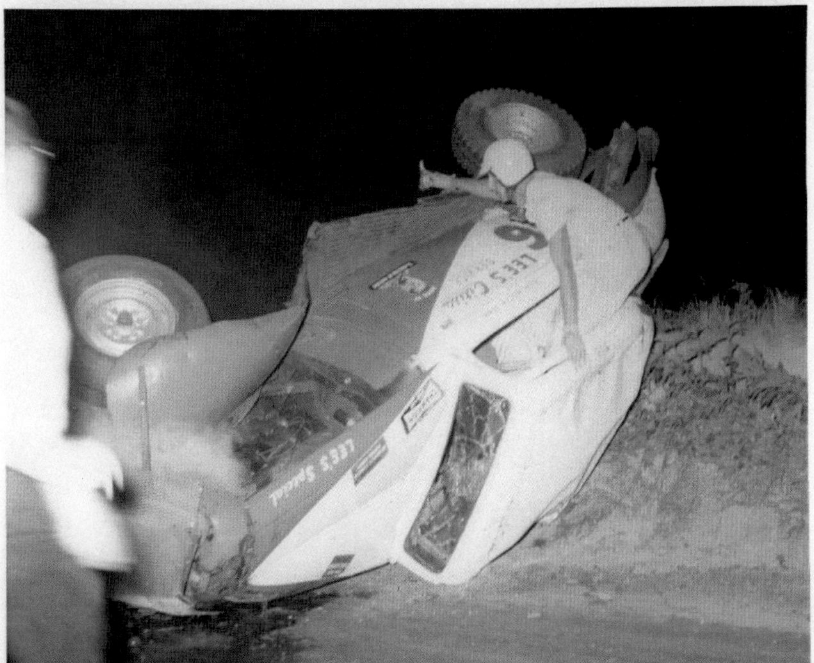
LEE'S Special

46

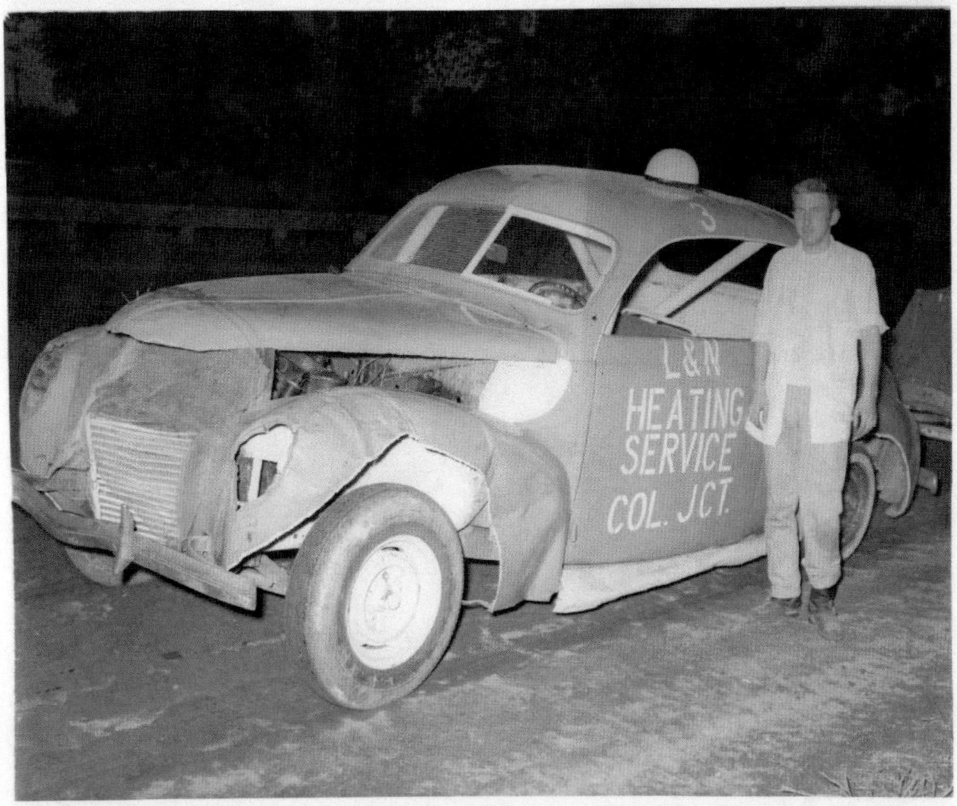
3
L&N
HEATING
SERVICE
COL. JCT.

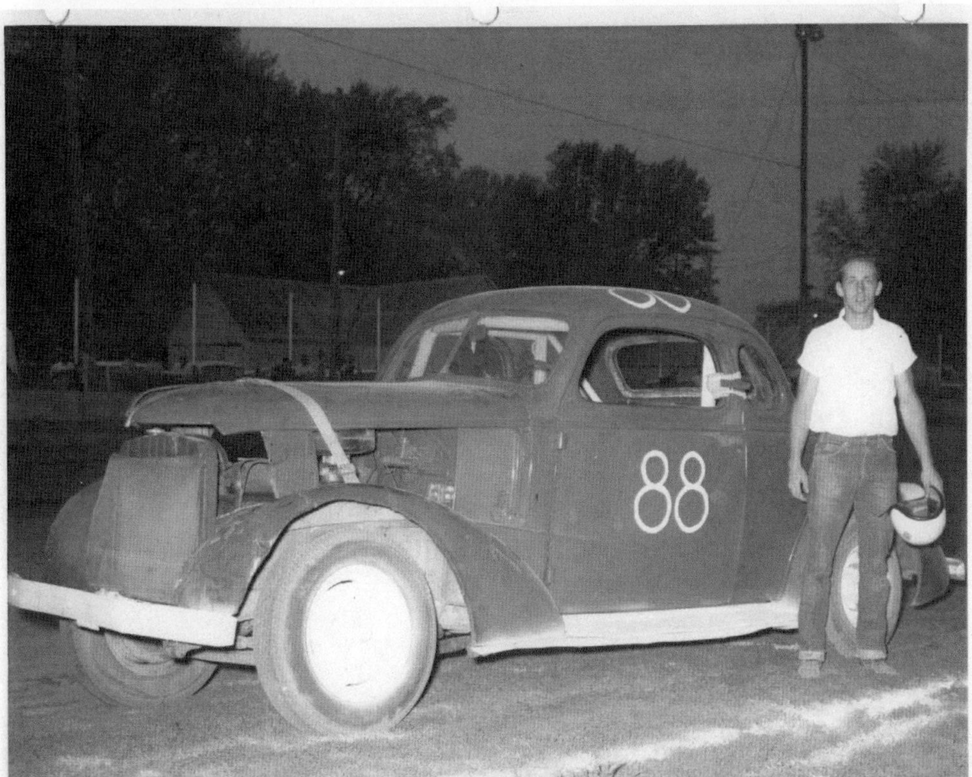
88

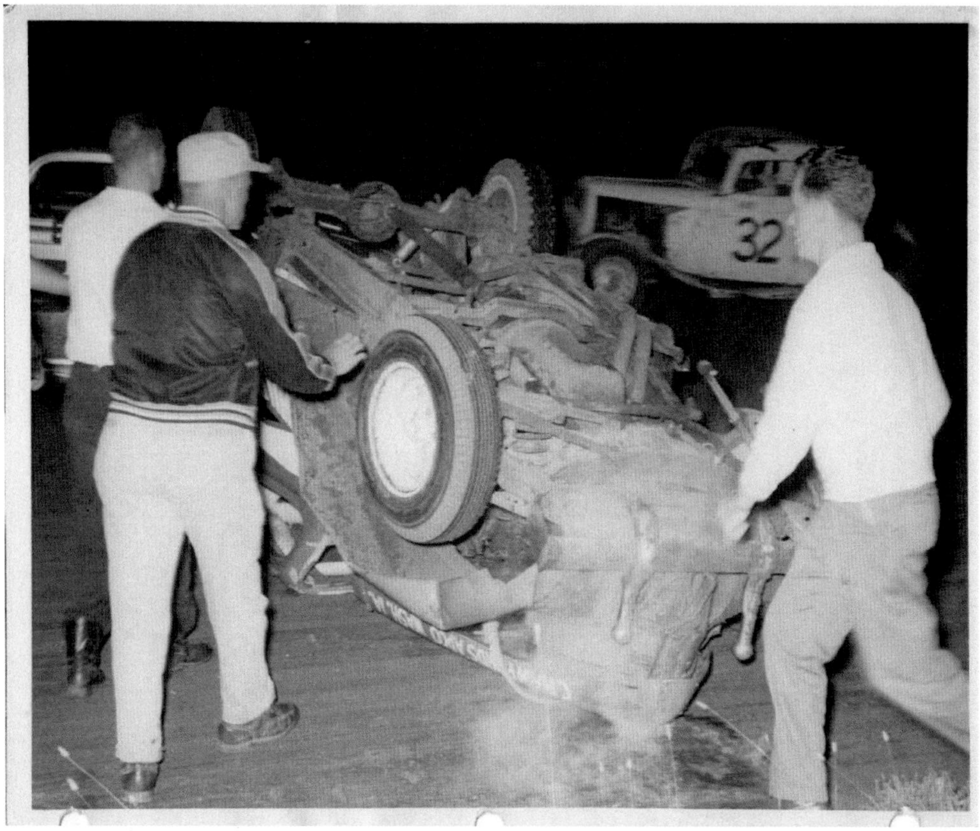
32

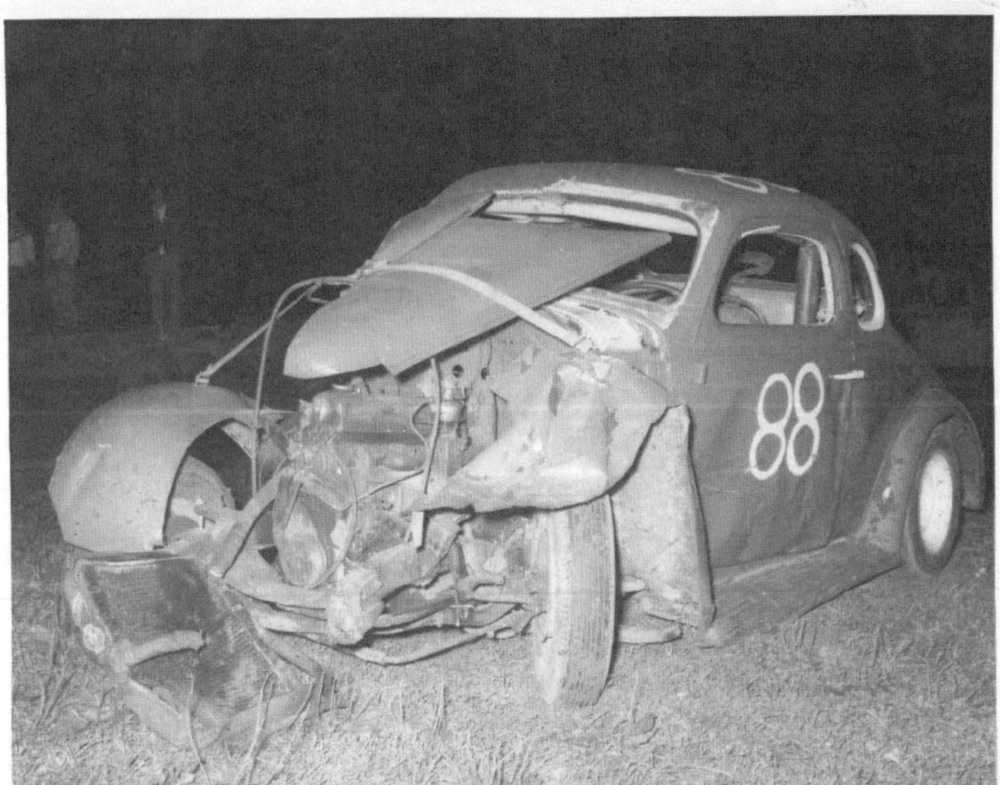
88

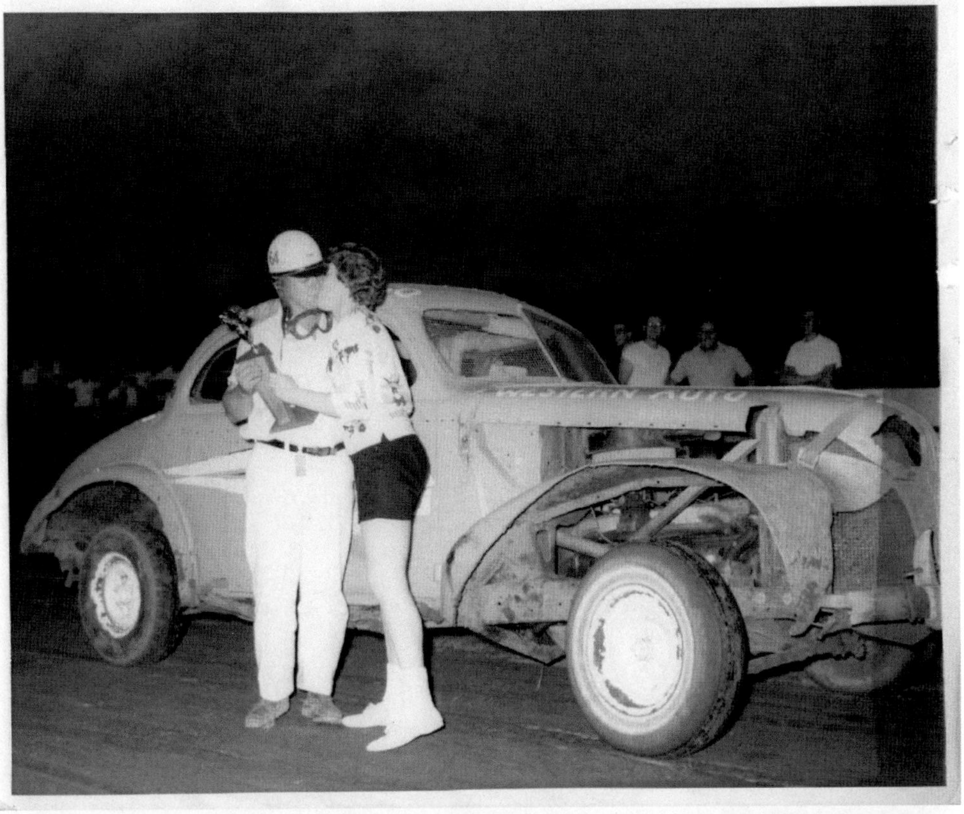

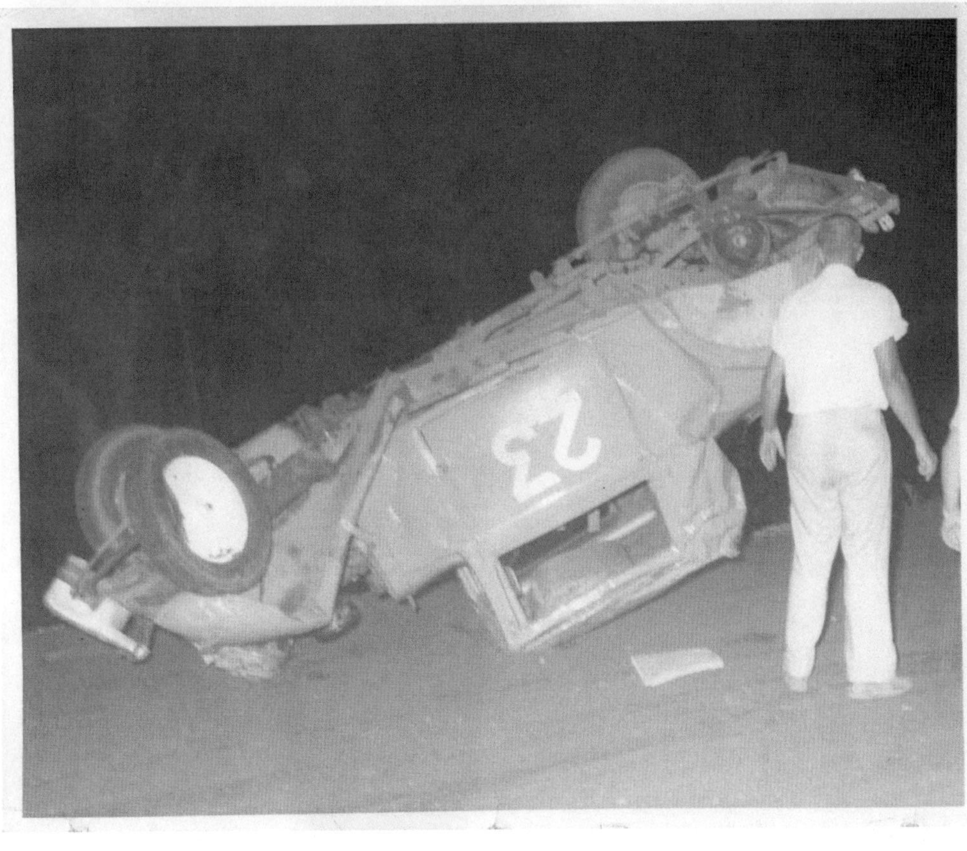
23

50

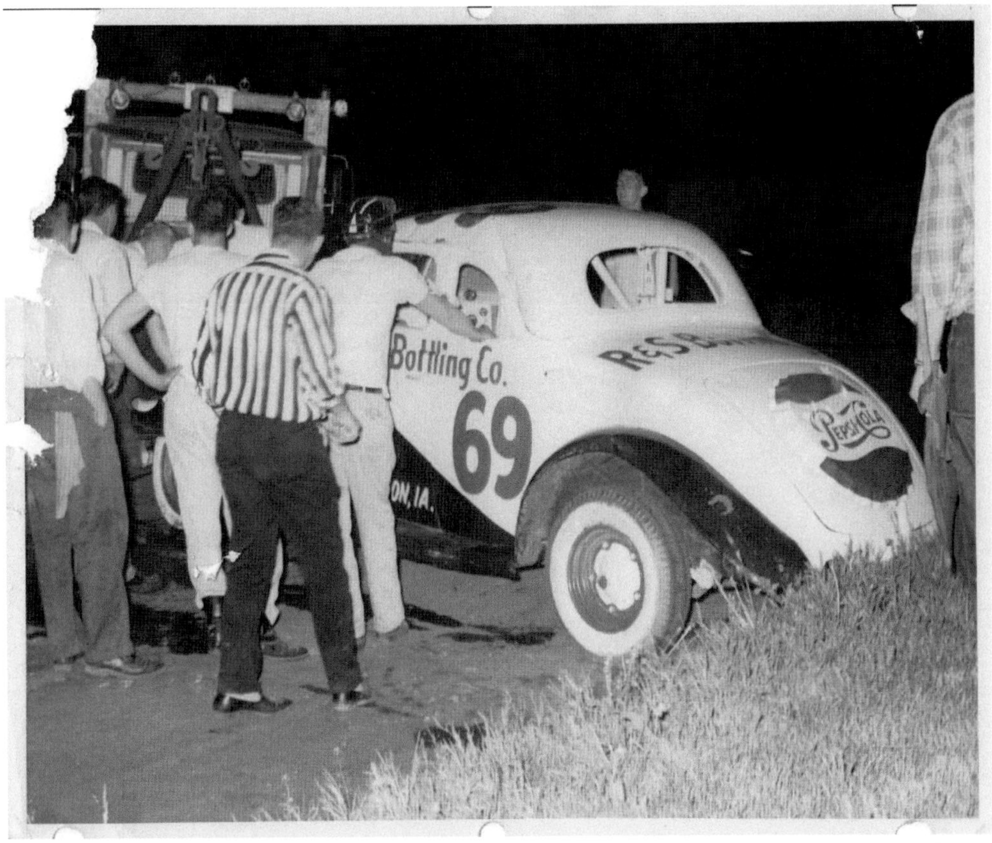
Bottling Co.
69
Pepsi-Cola

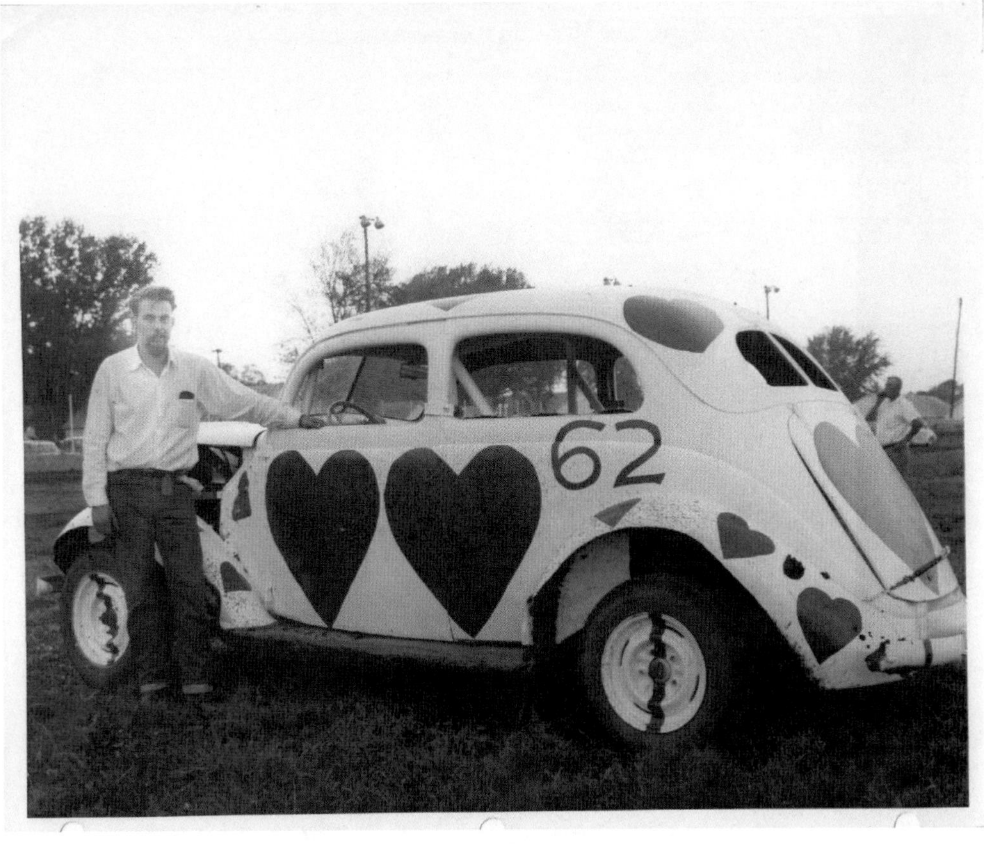
62

62
BIERMAN'S
REPAIR SHOP
TRACTOR REPAIR
MUSCATINE

AGENCY OIL CO.
49
BURLINGTON IA.

53

54

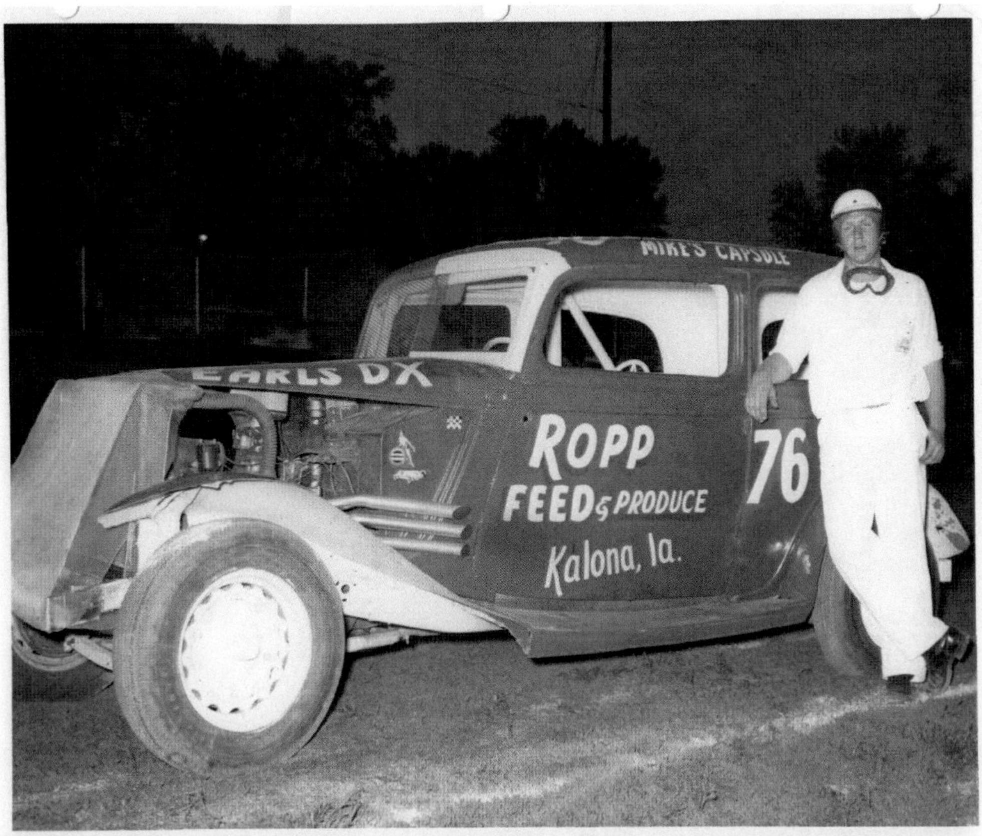
MIKE'S CAPSULE
EARLS DX
ROPP
FEED & PRODUCE
Kalona, Ia.
76

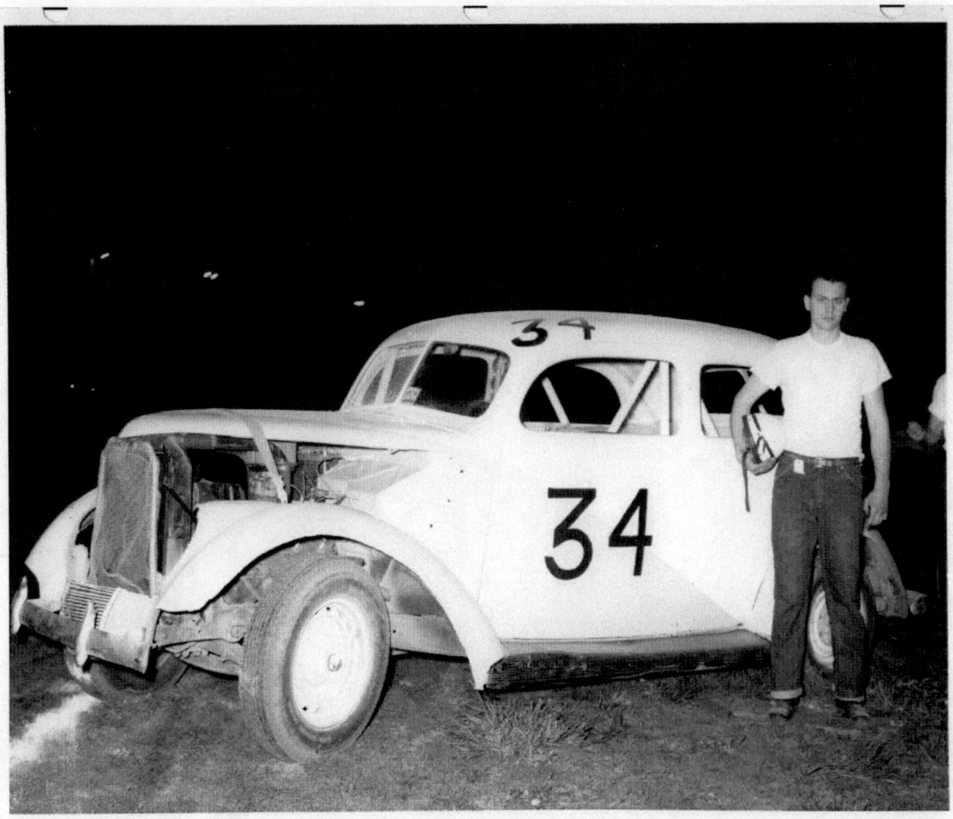
34
34

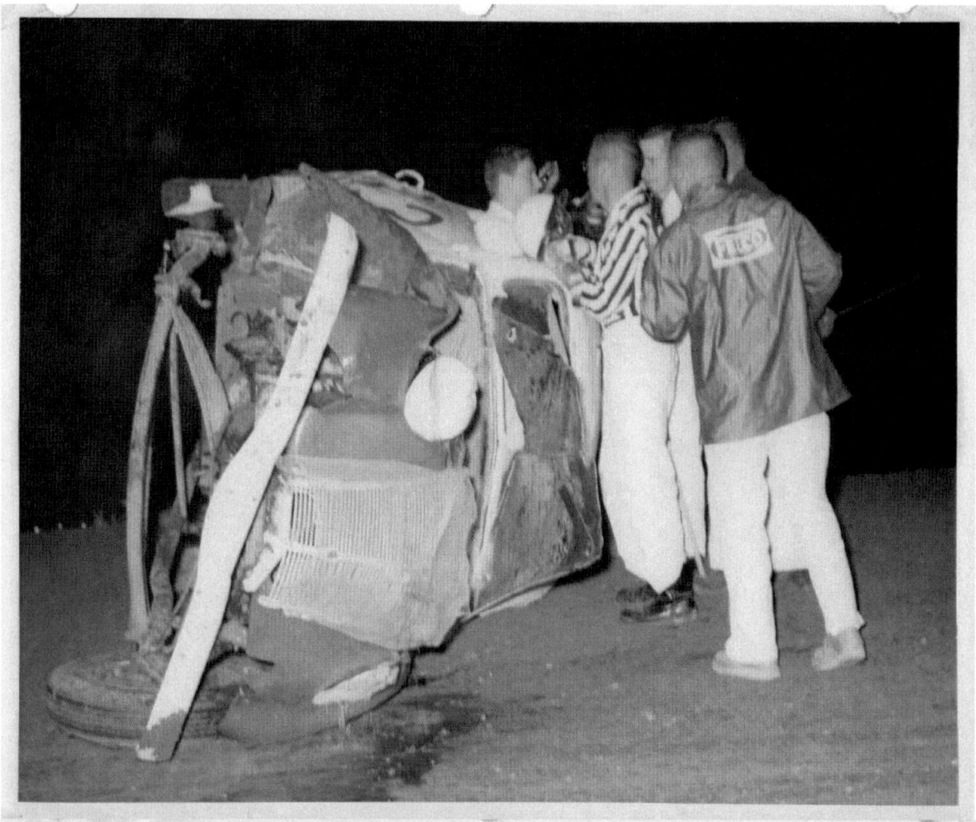

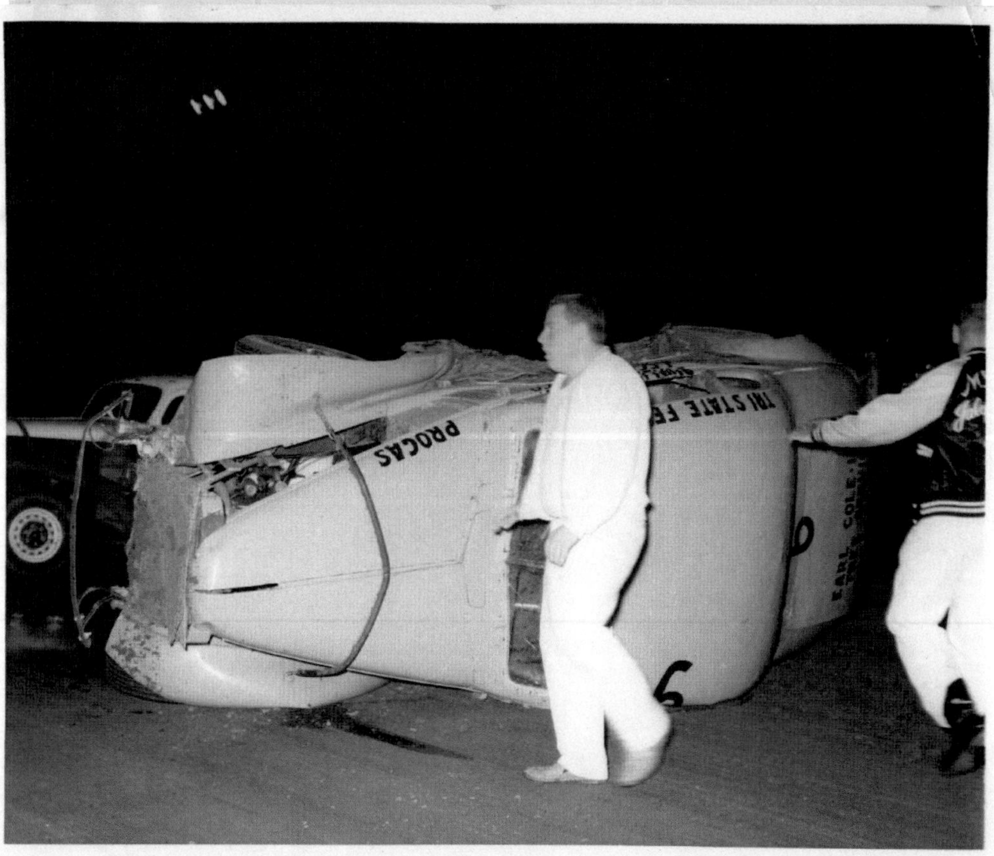
PROCAS
TRI STATE

57

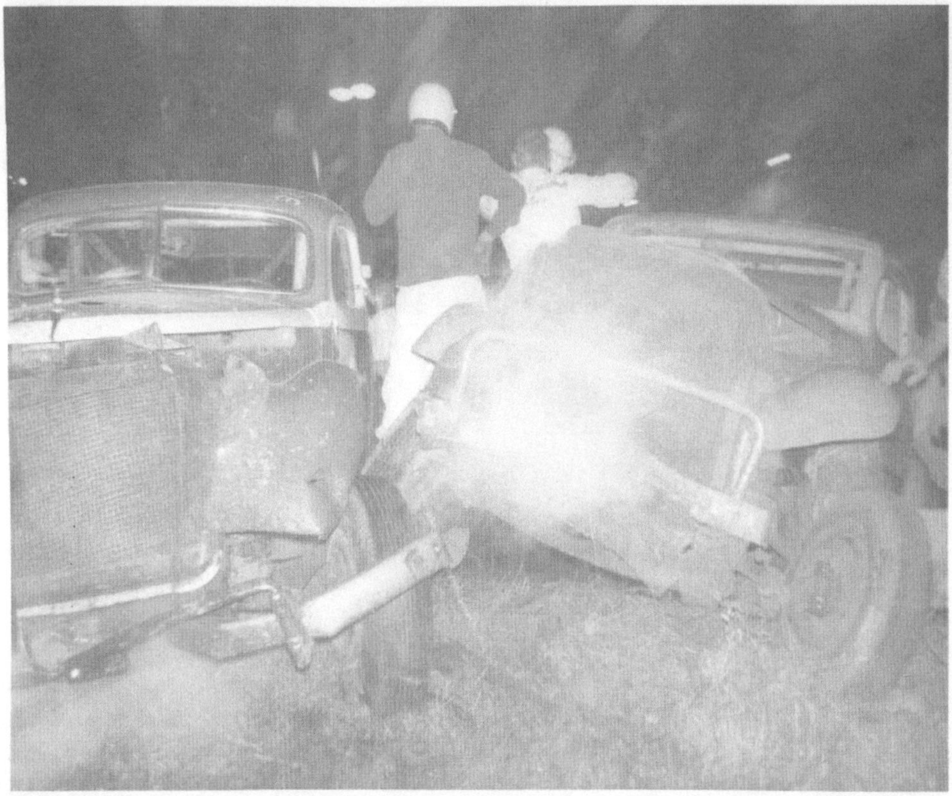

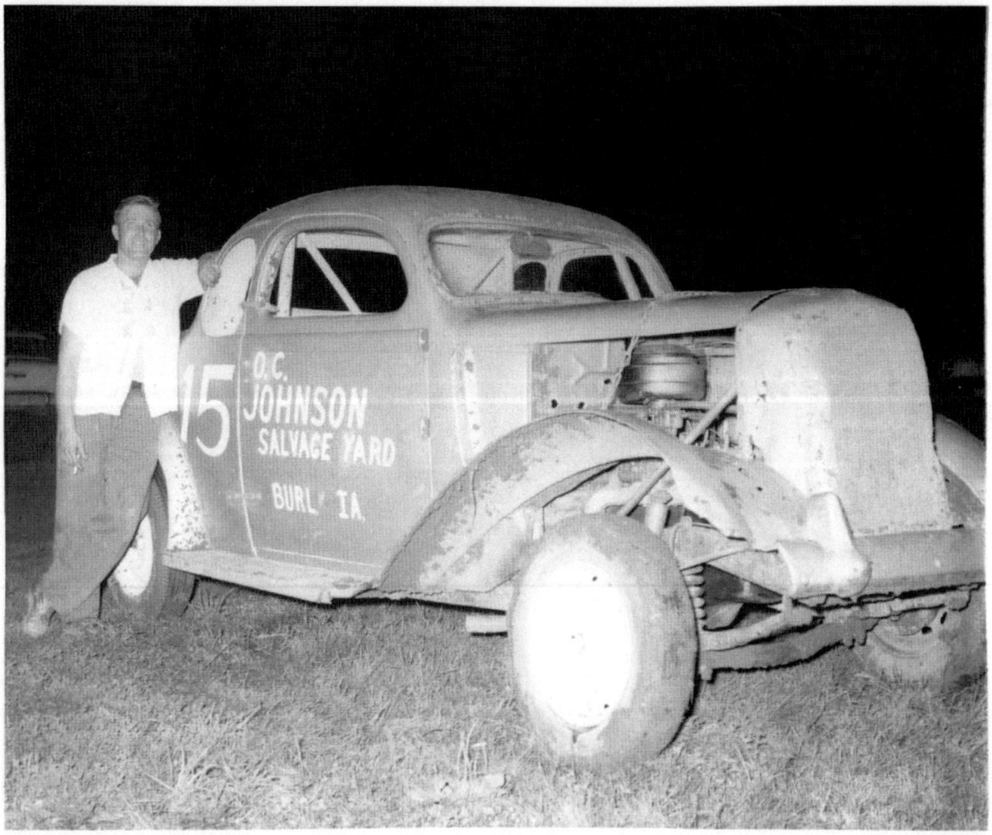
15
O.C.
JOHNSON
SALVAGE YARD
BURL IA.

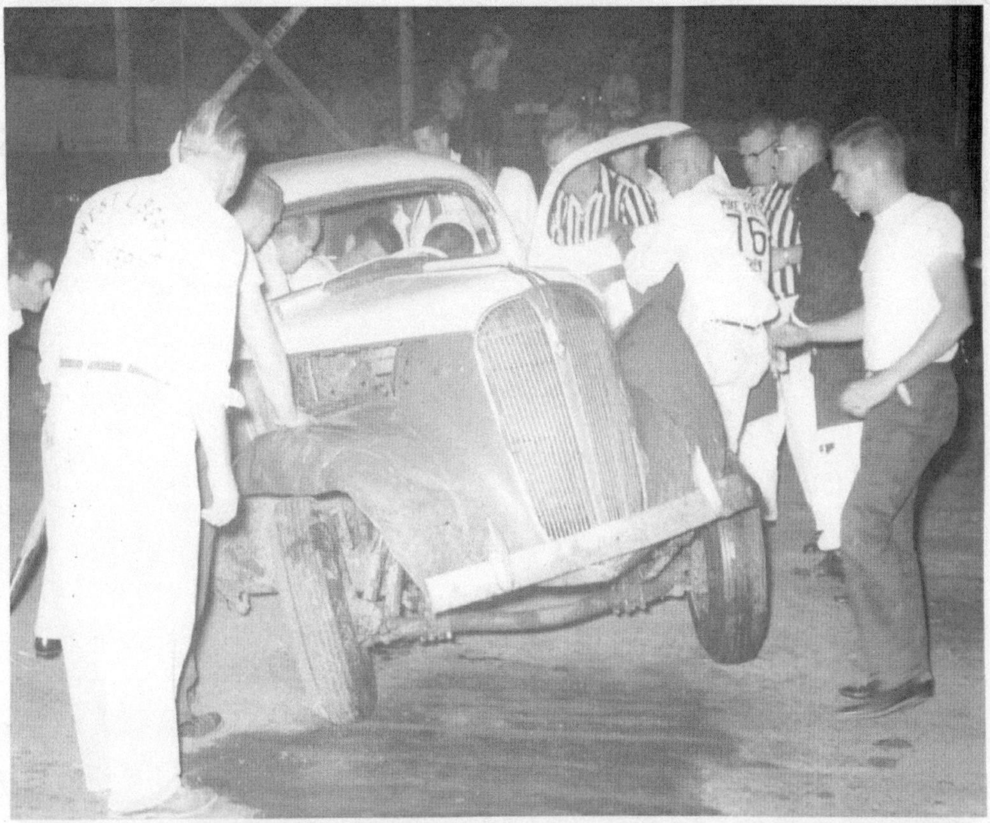
76

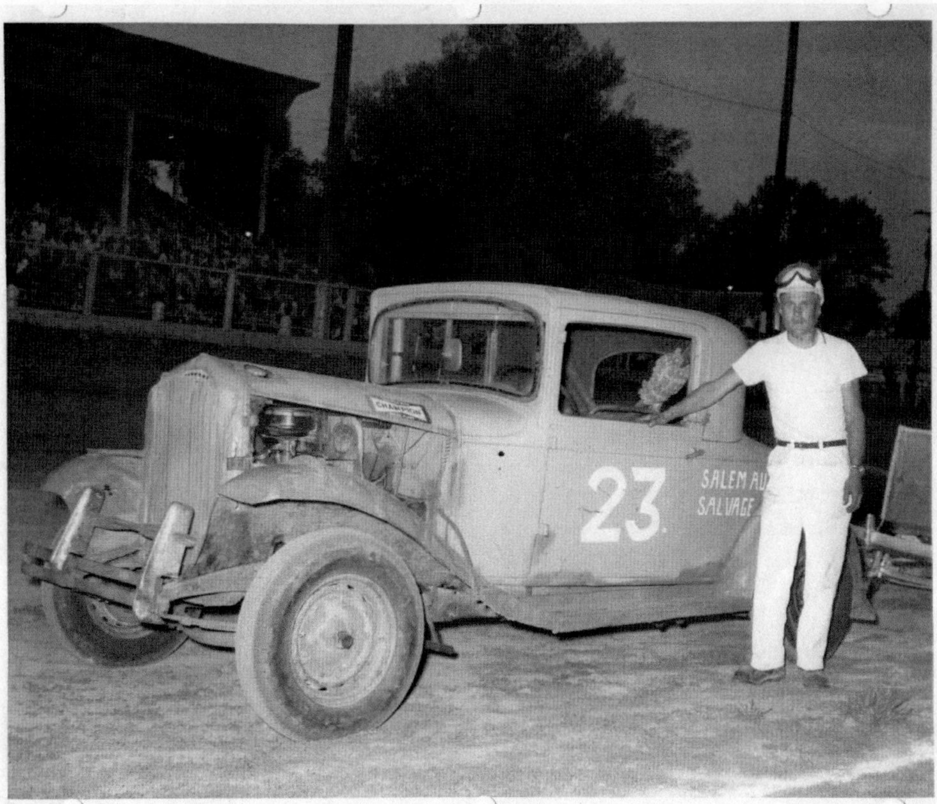
23.
SALEM AU
SALVAGE

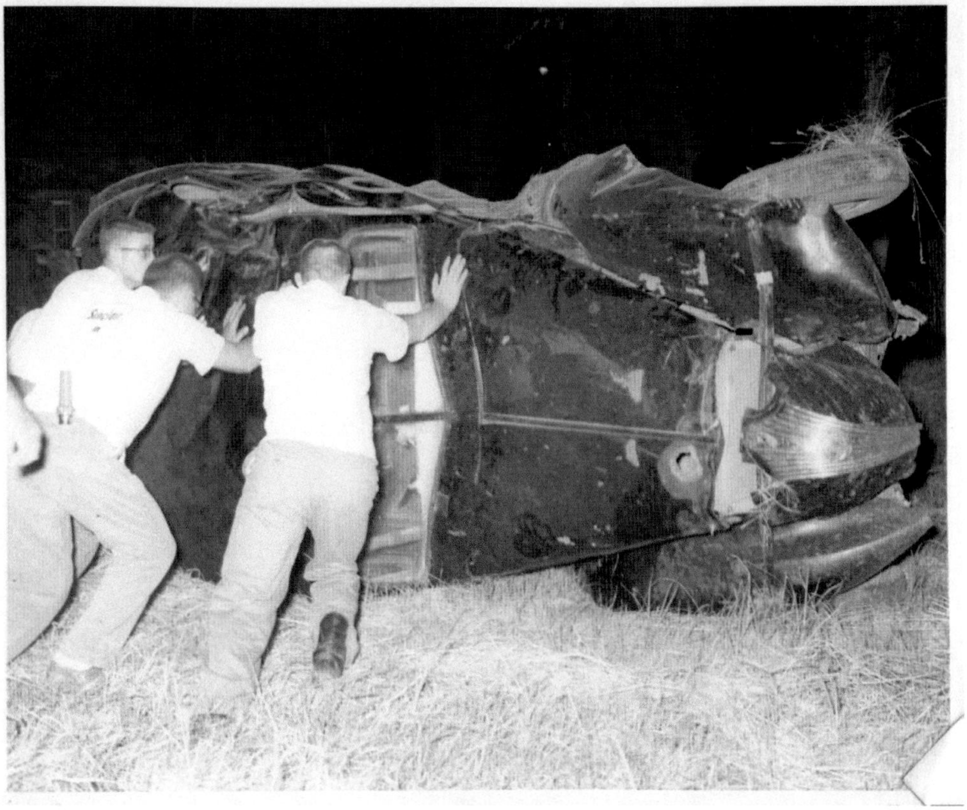

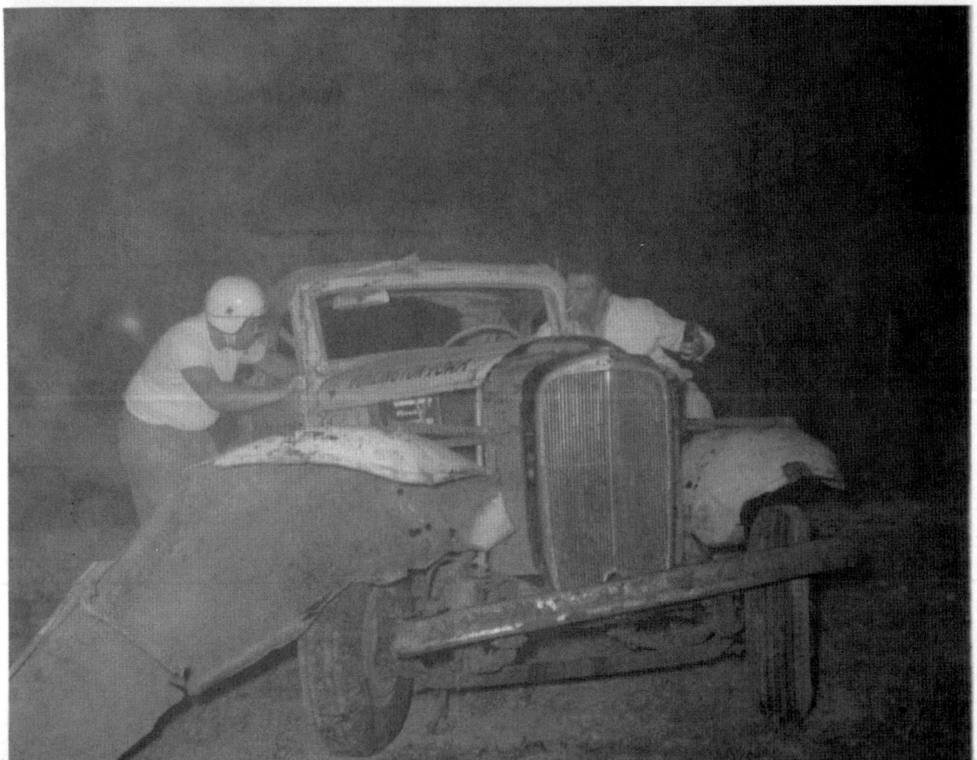

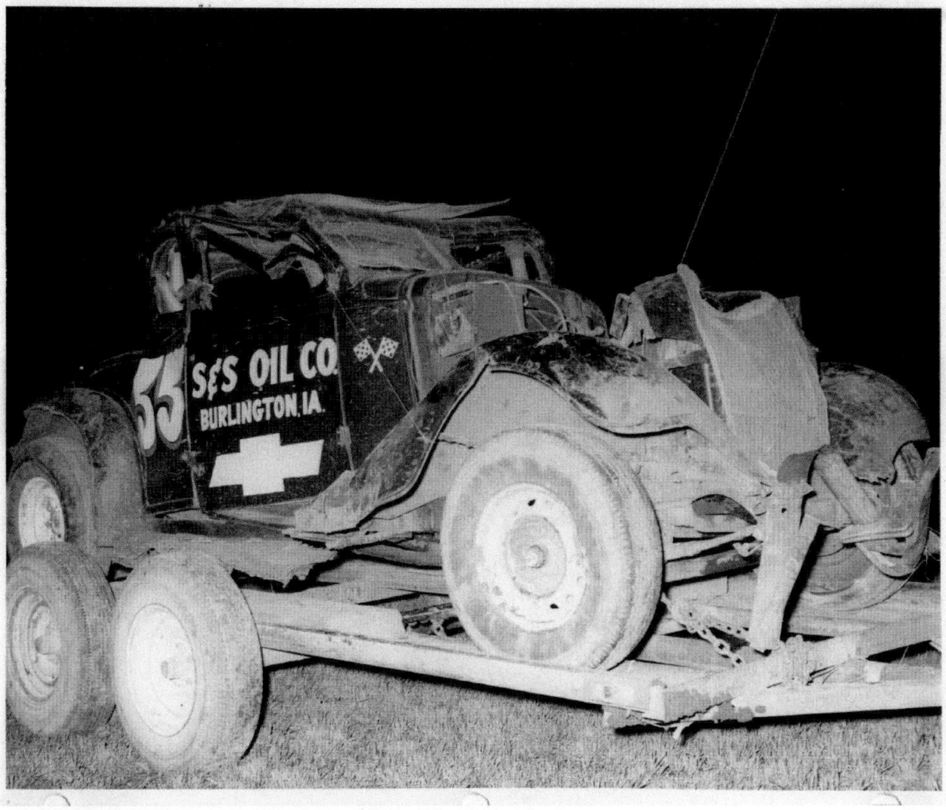
53
S&S OIL CO.
BURLINGTON, IA.

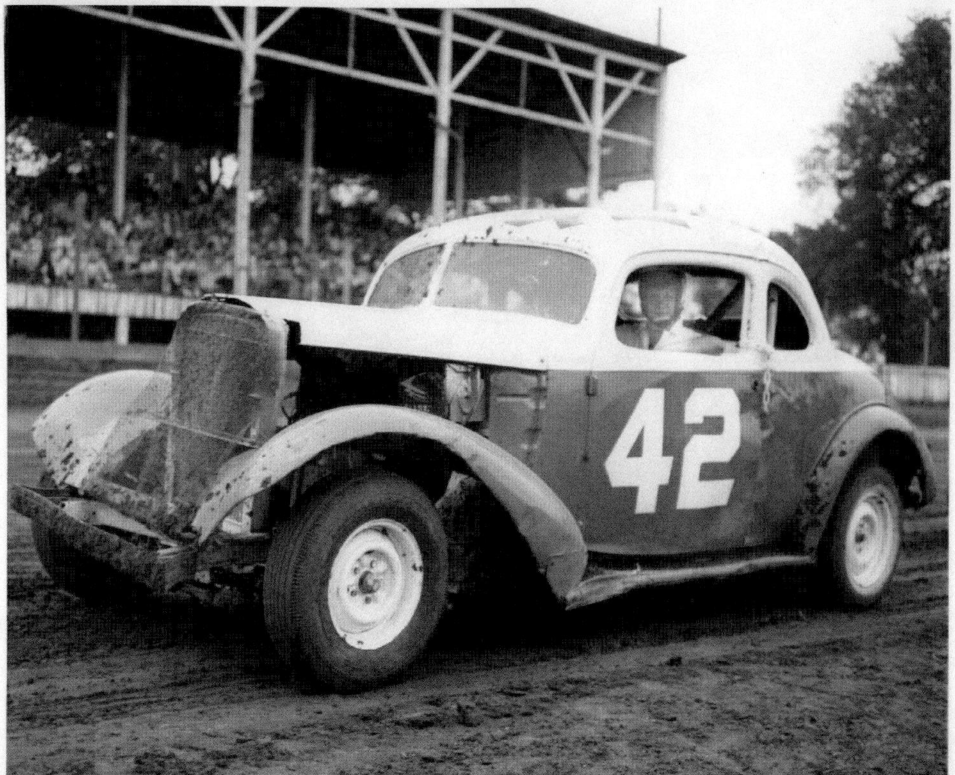
42

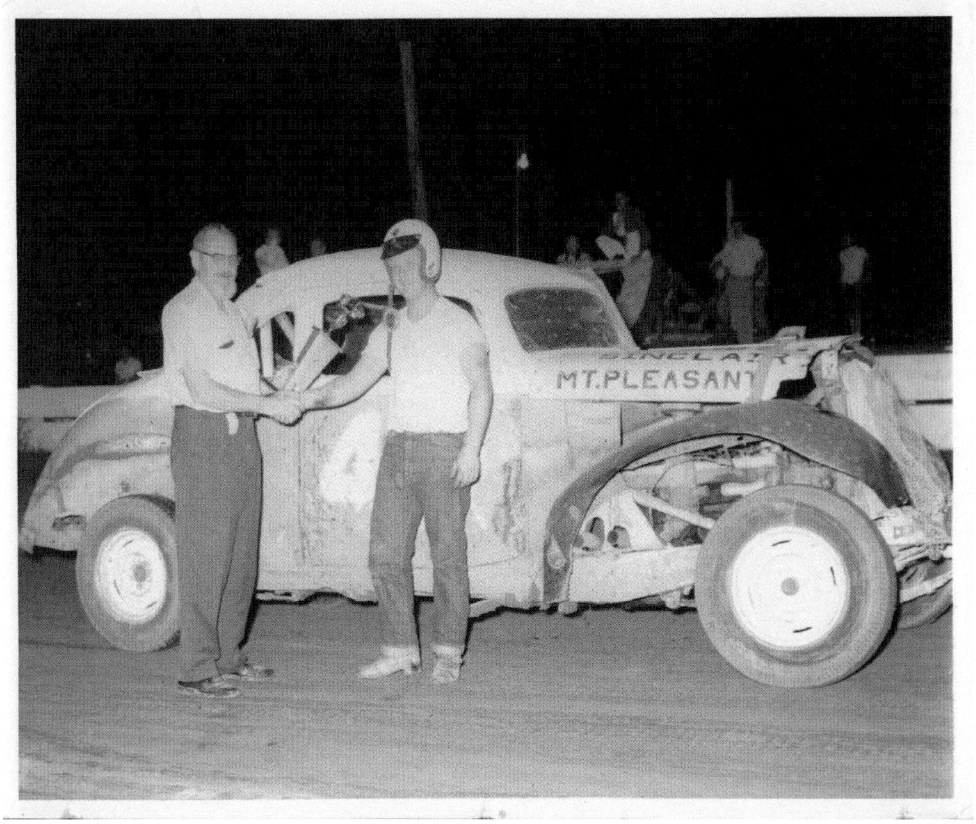
MT.PLEASANT

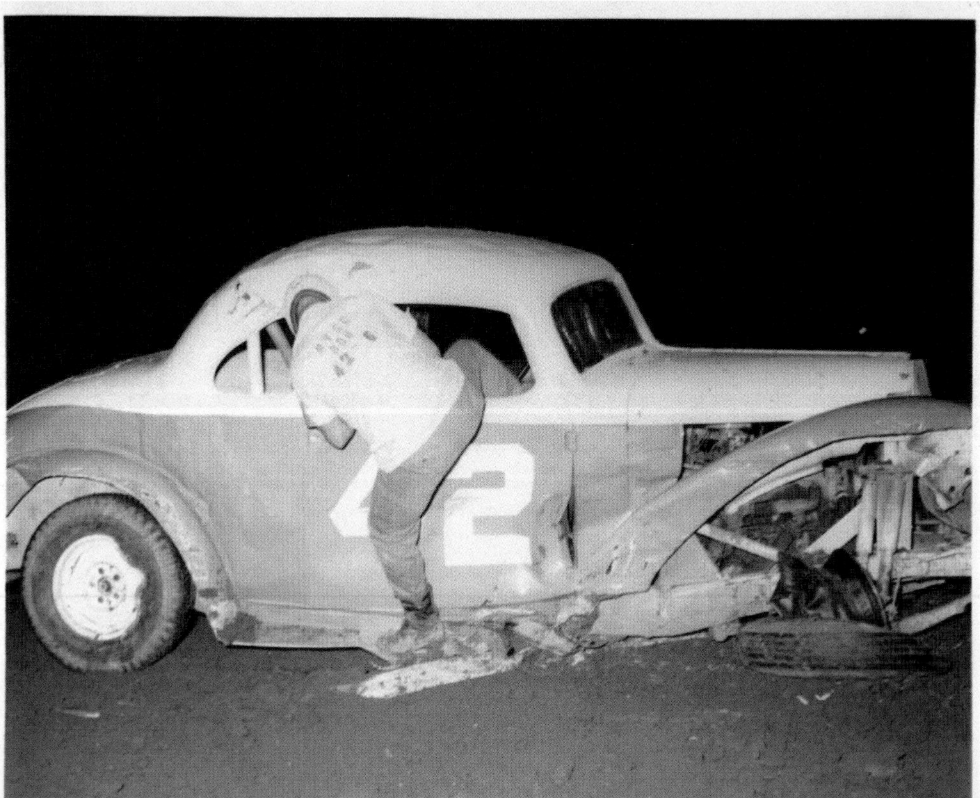
42

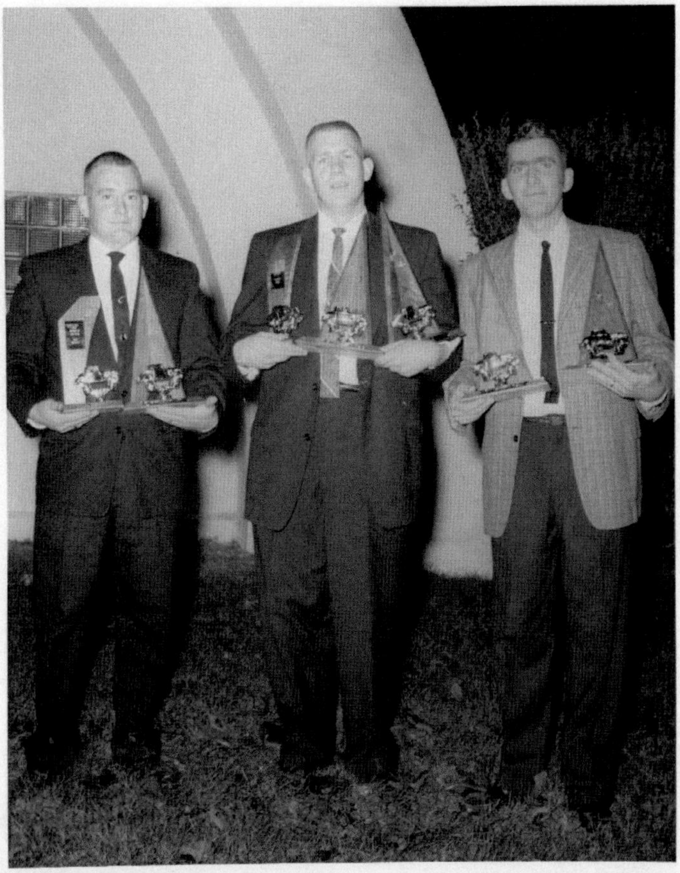

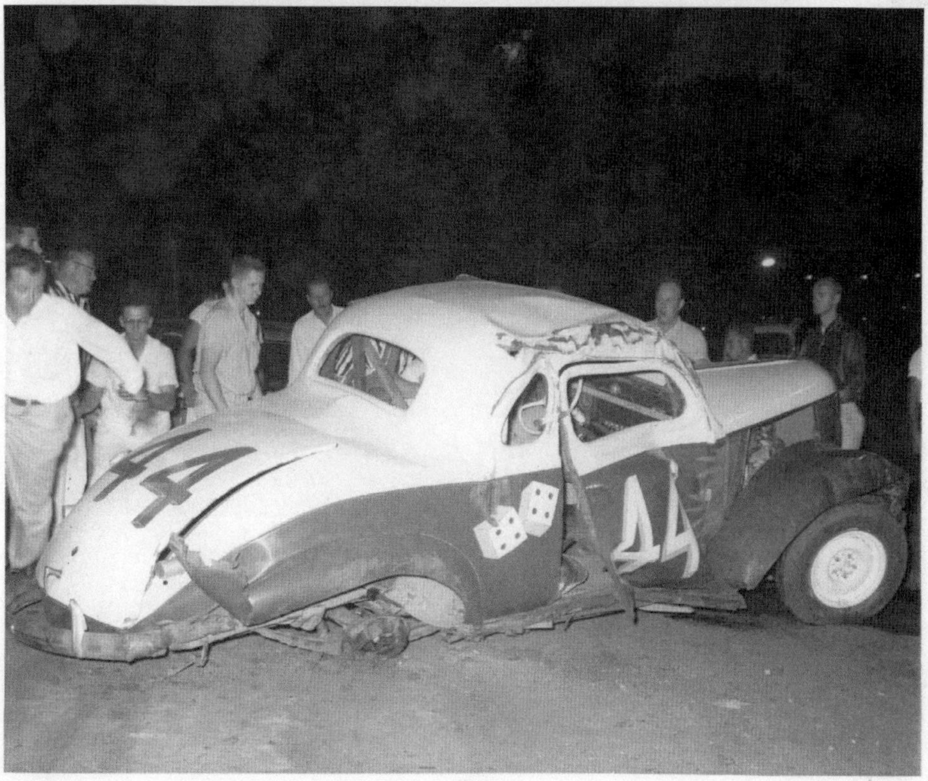
44
44

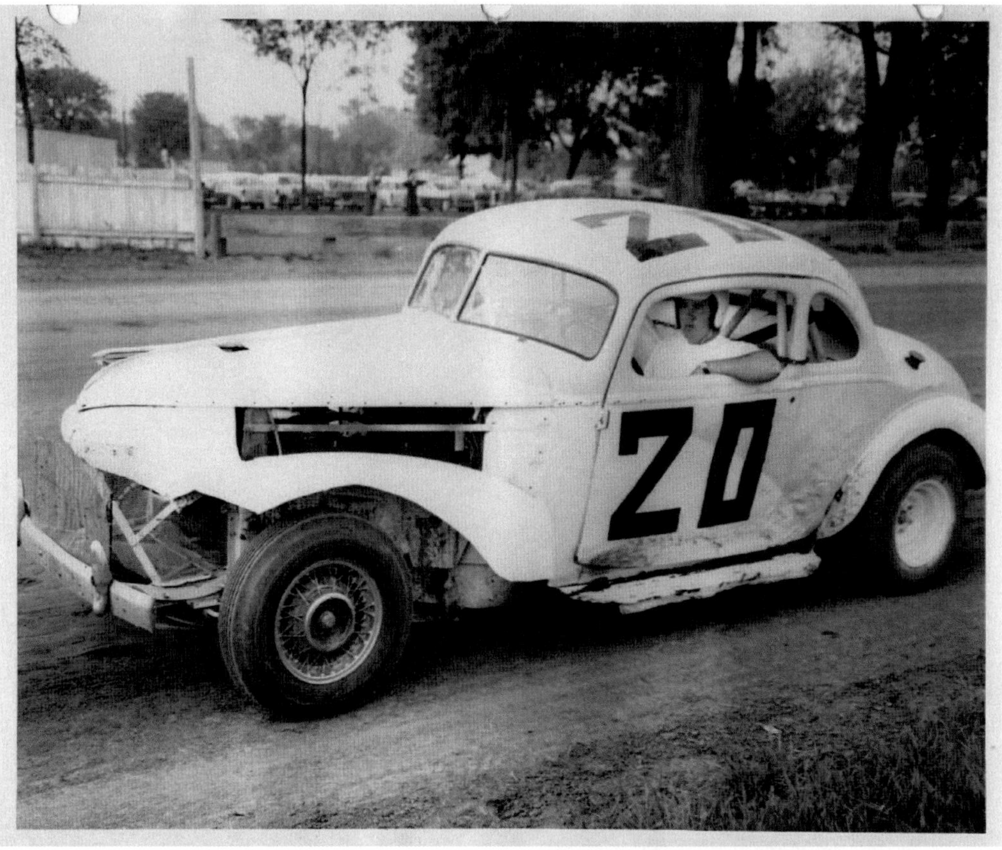
20

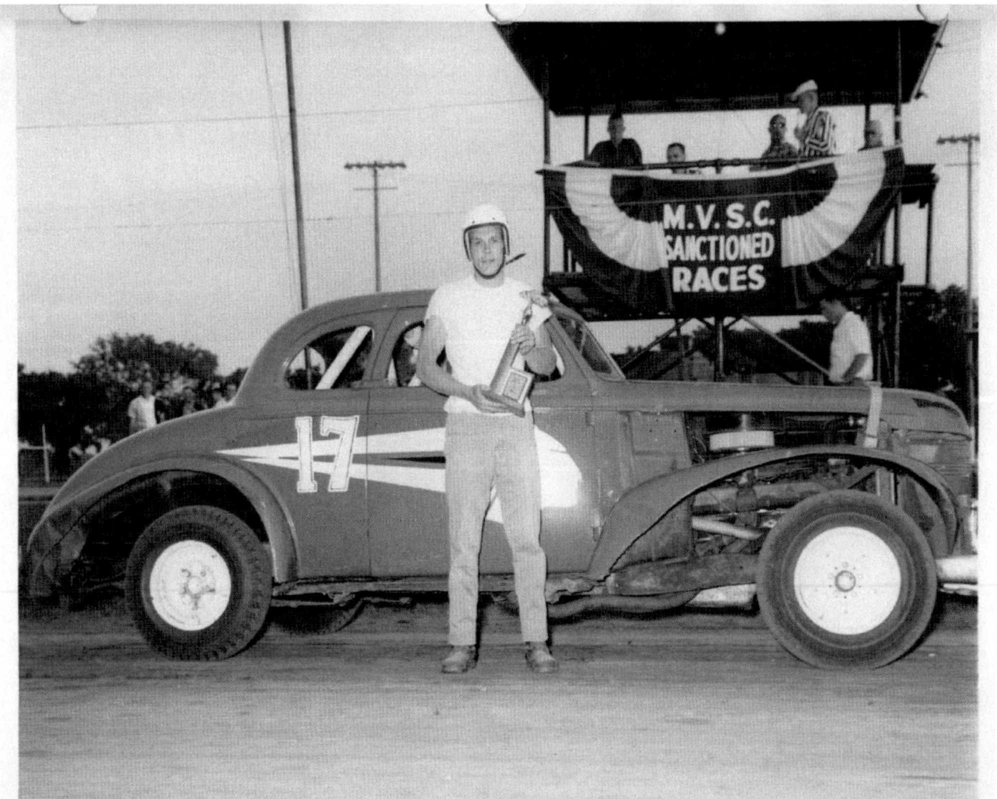
M.V.S.C.
SANCTIONED
RACES
17

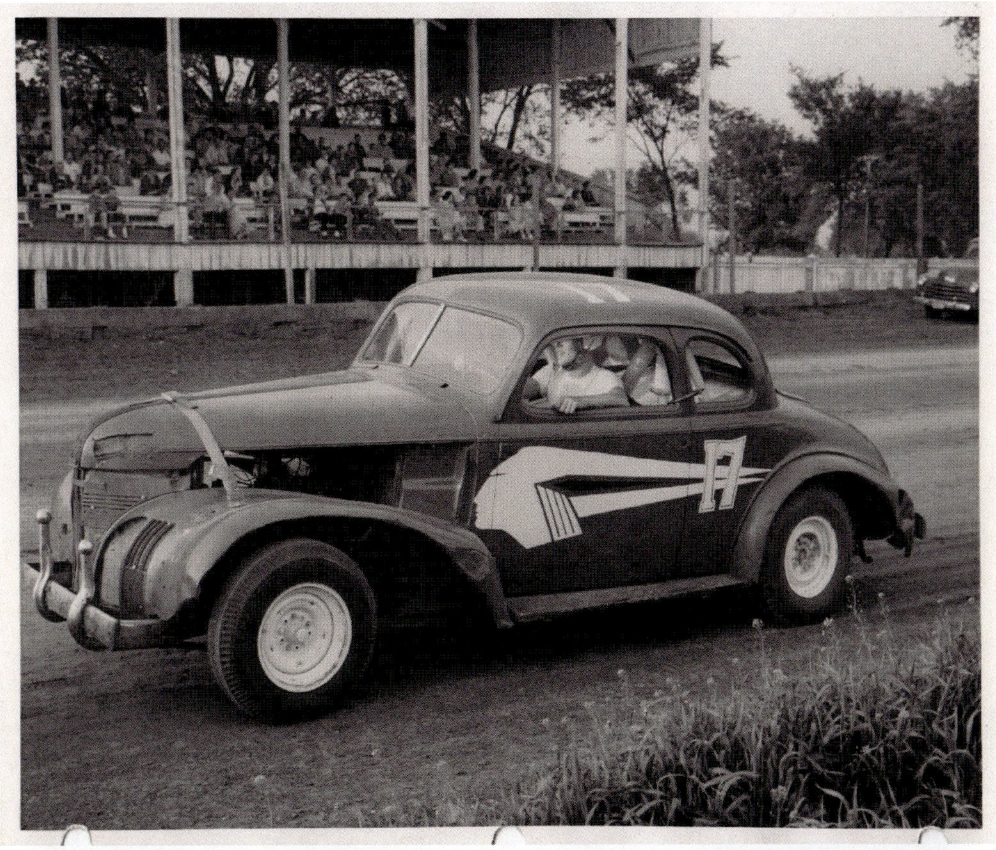
17

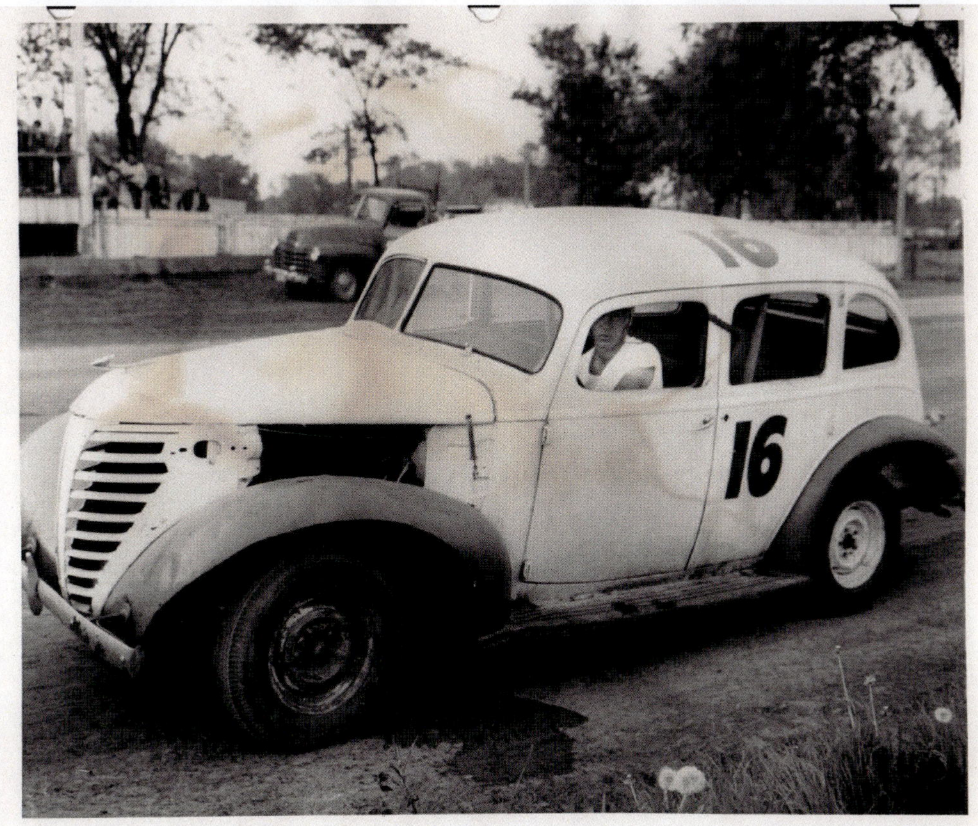
16
16

66

W BURL
WALNUT
CO.
15

MOBIL Service
11
Fisher
Motors
Columbus
Jct
PONTIAC
GMC

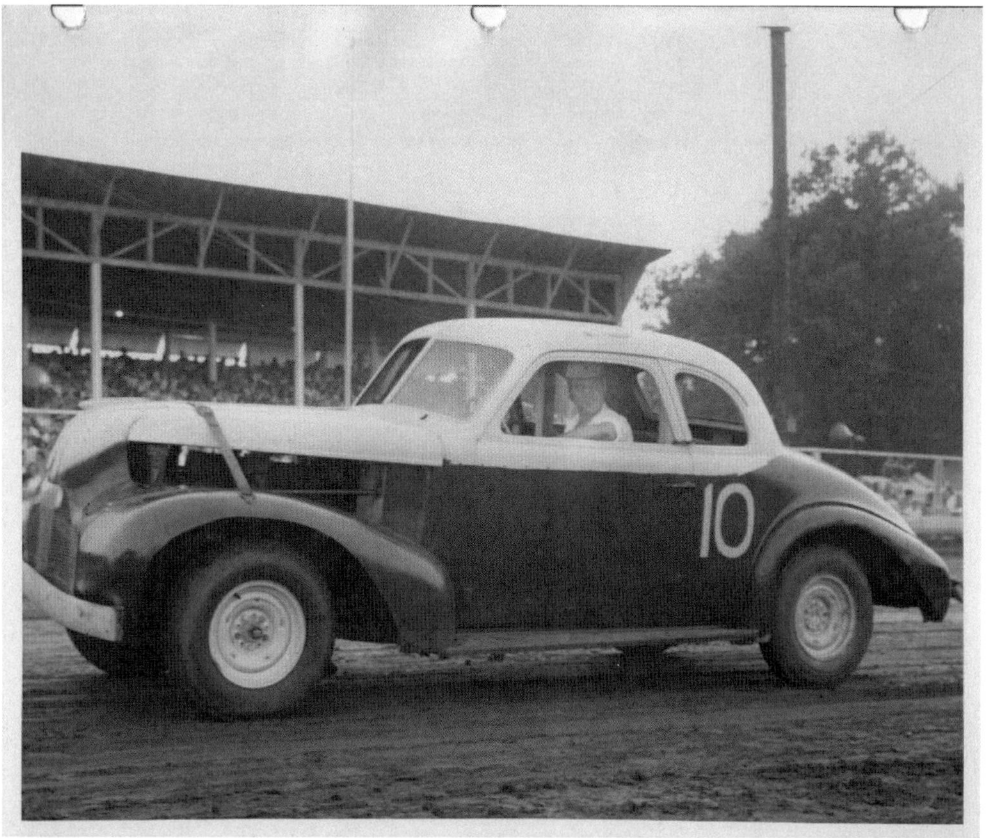
10

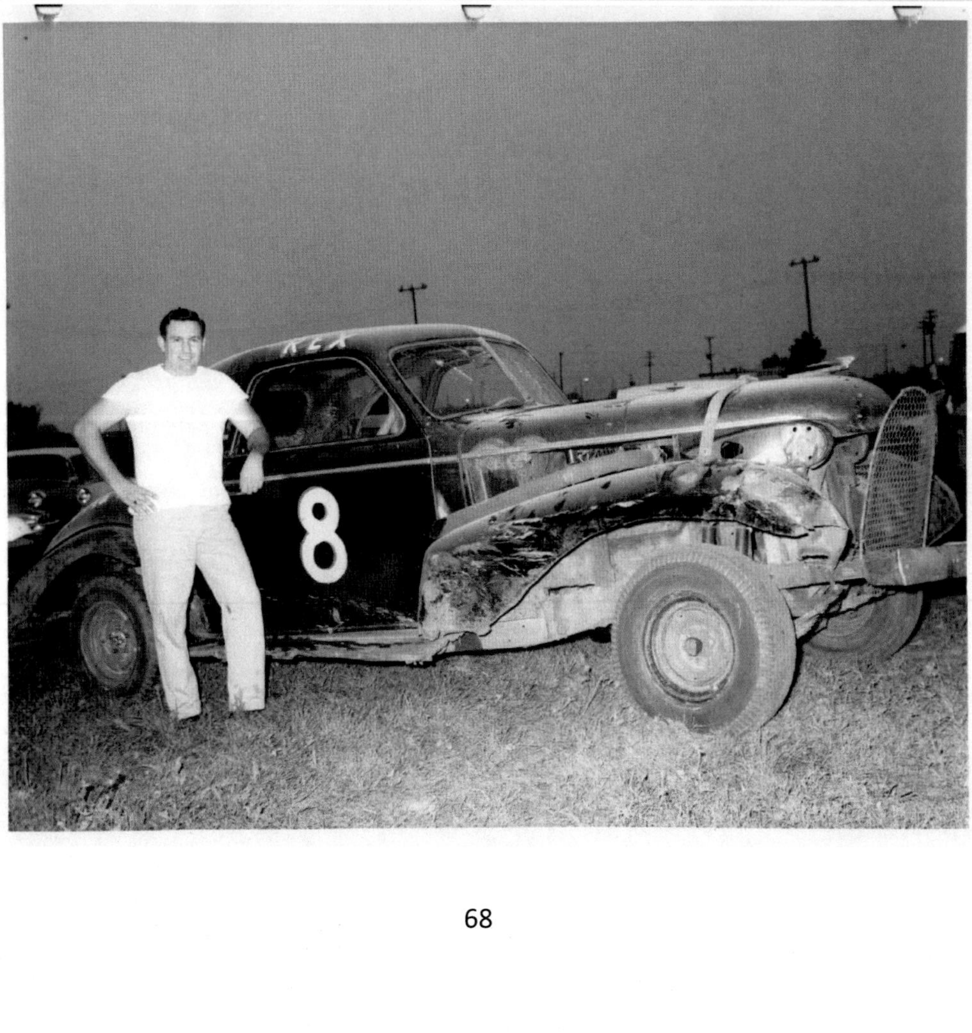
8

6
BOB
HAIGHTS
TIRES

2
MT. PLEASANT
WILCOX
WELDING
2
PHONE 653
HELIARC WELDING
PORTABLE ELECTRIC & ACETYLENE

WEST LIBERTY
SMITTY'S
FORD
SALES

M.V.S.C.
SANCTIONED
BURLINGTON IOWA
OAK-OSBORN
BURLINGTON IOWA

BURLINGTON IOWA
WHITEY'S-SINCLAIR-SERVICE
OAK-OSBORN
BURLINGTON IOWA

17

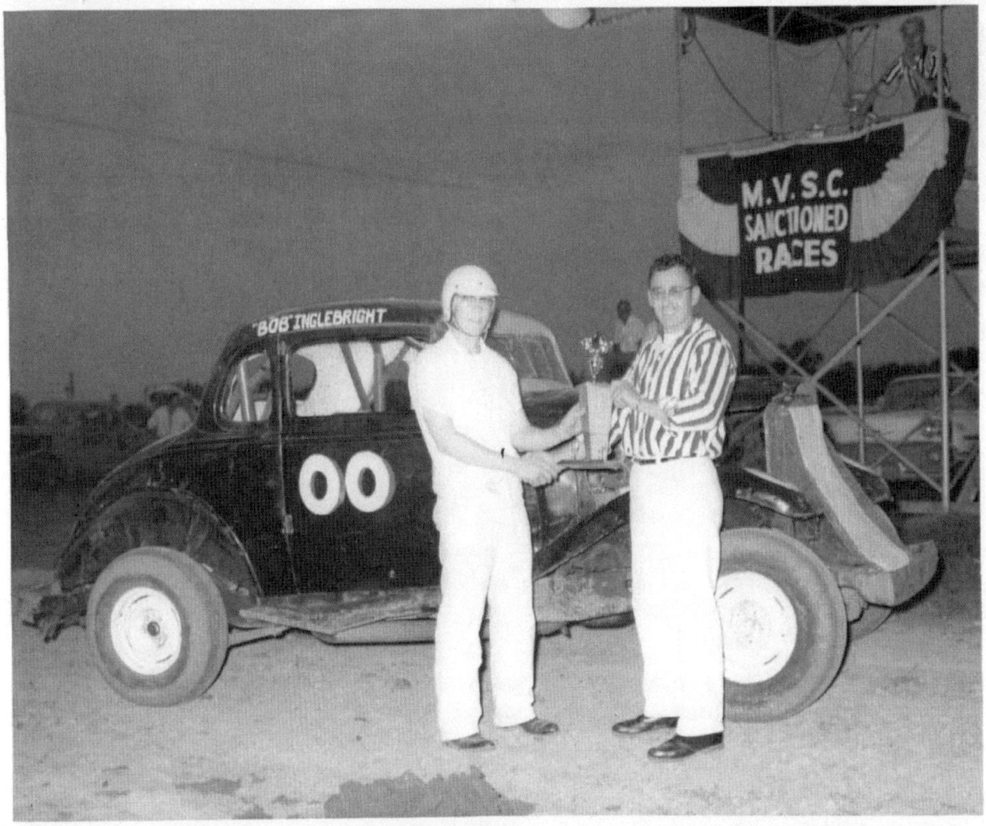
"BOB" INGLEBRIGHT
00
M.V.S.C.
SANCTIONED
RACES

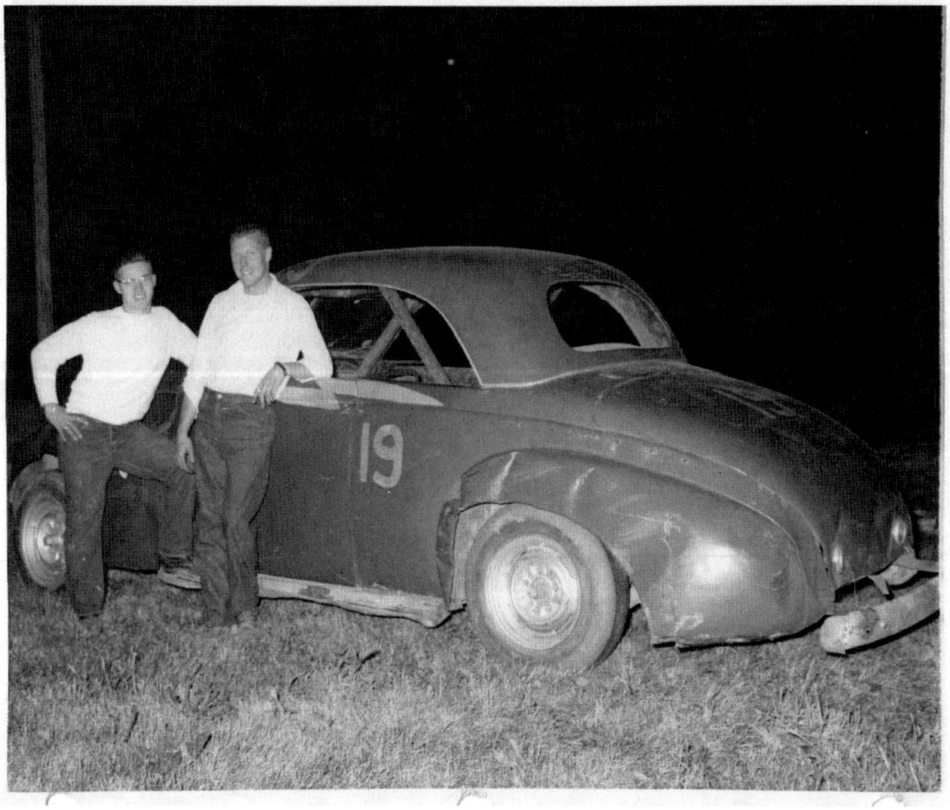
19

73

74

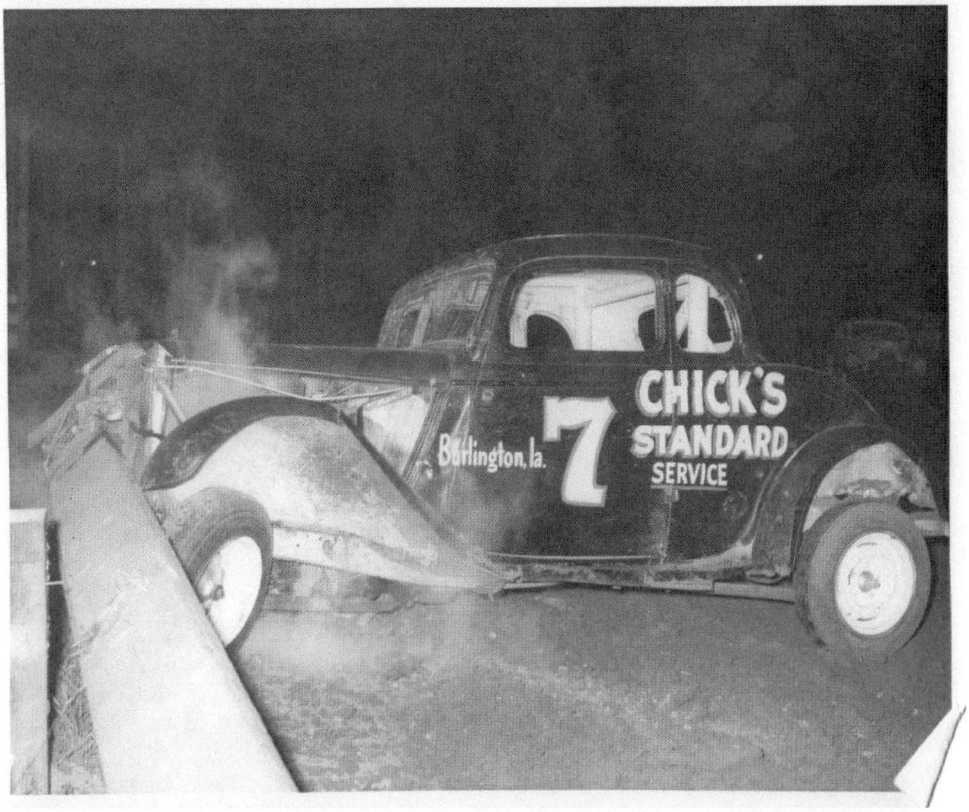
Burlington, Ia.
7
CHICK'S
STANDARD
SERVICE

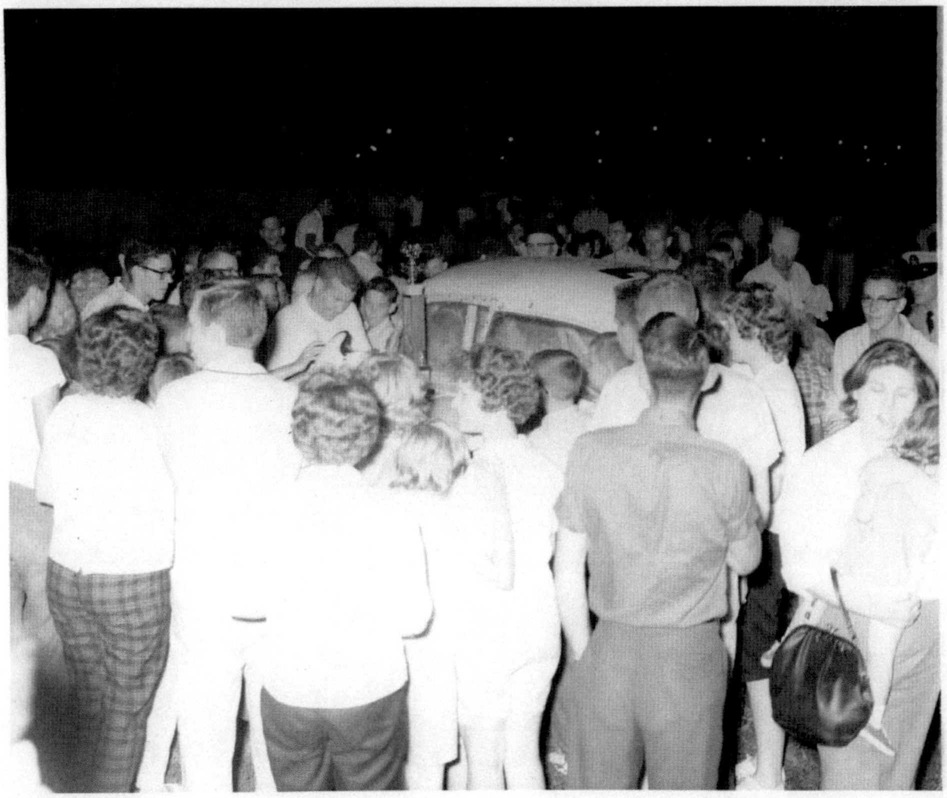

76

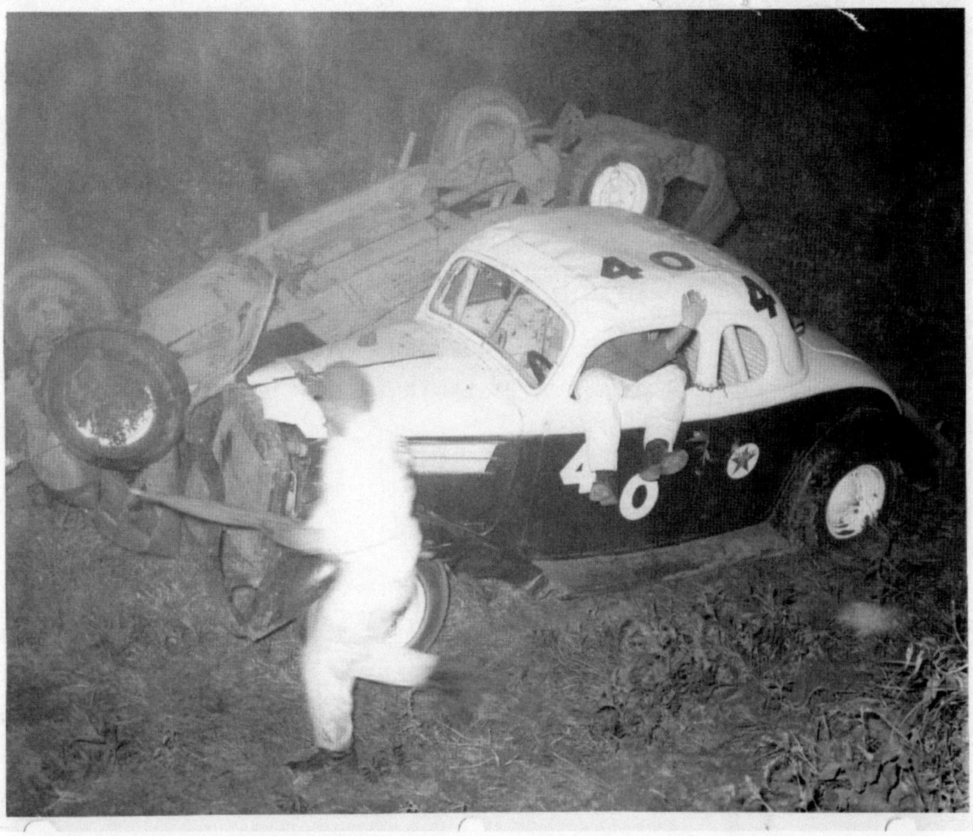
40
40

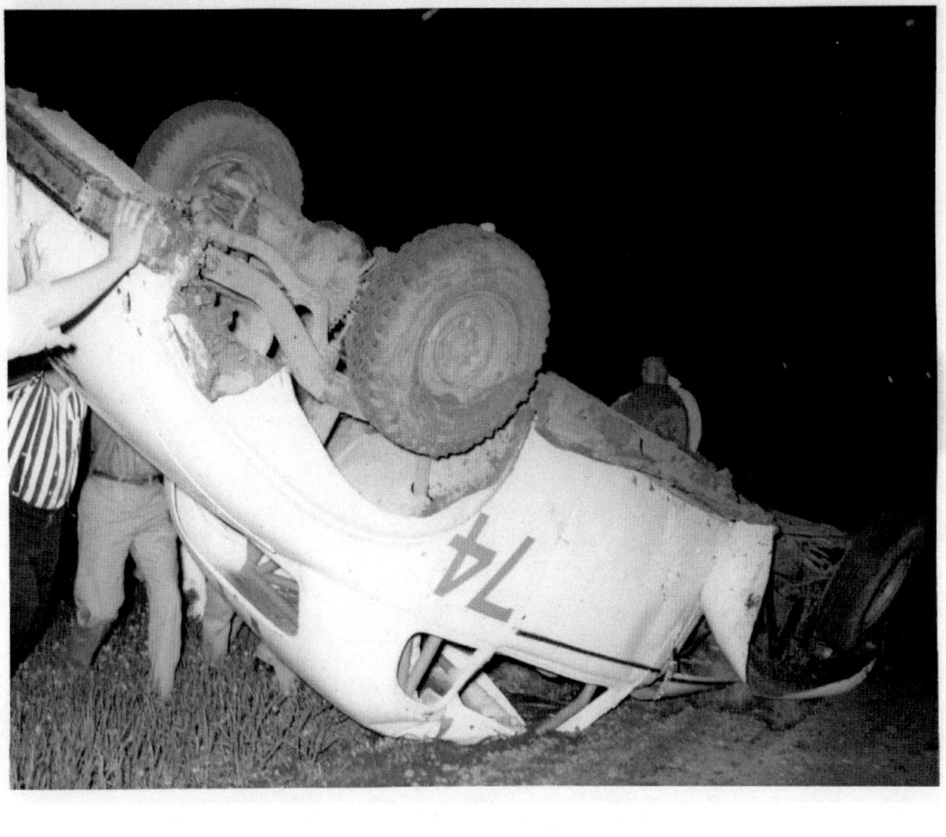
74

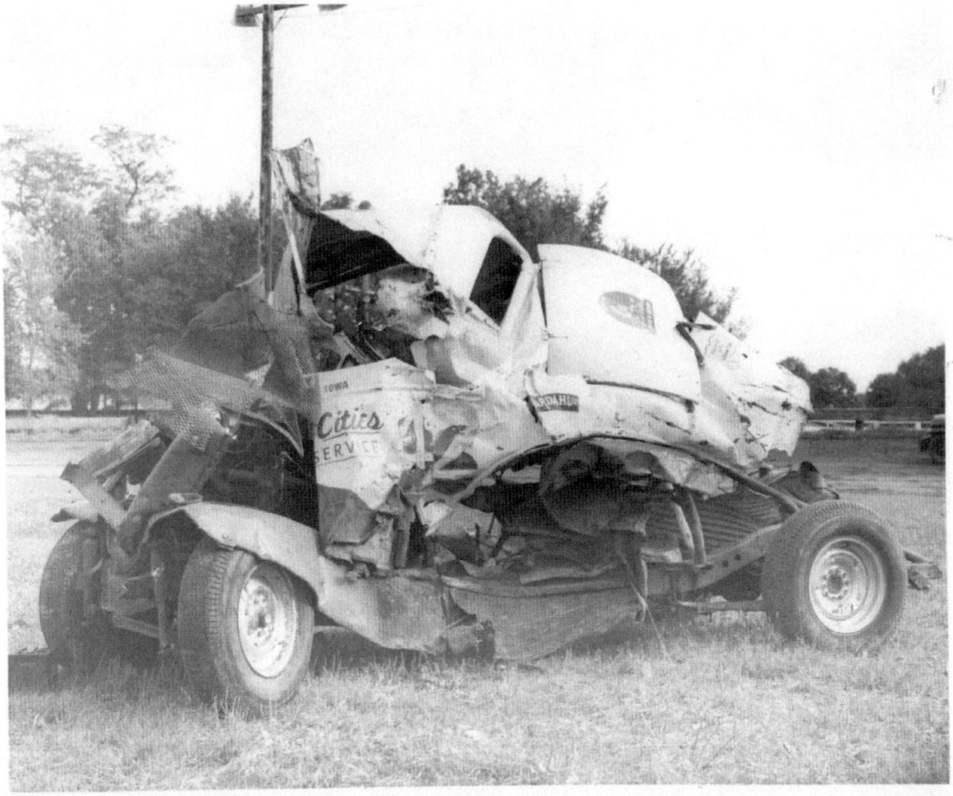
Cities
SERVICE

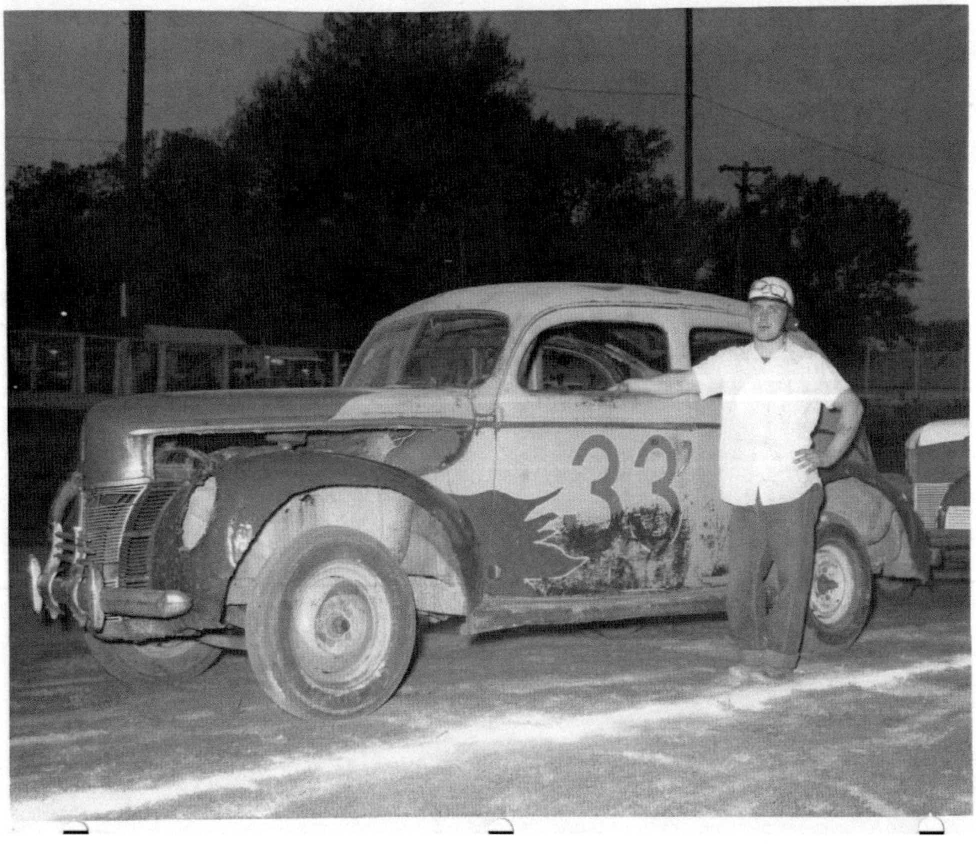
33

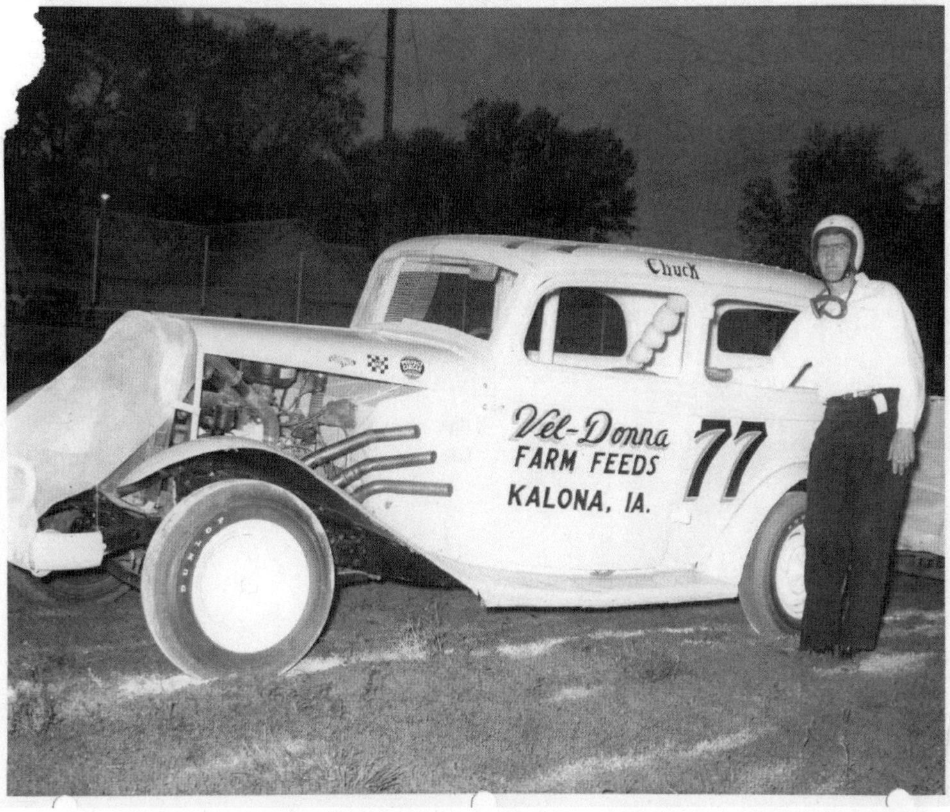
Chuck
Vel-Donna
FARM FEEDS
KALONA, IA.
77

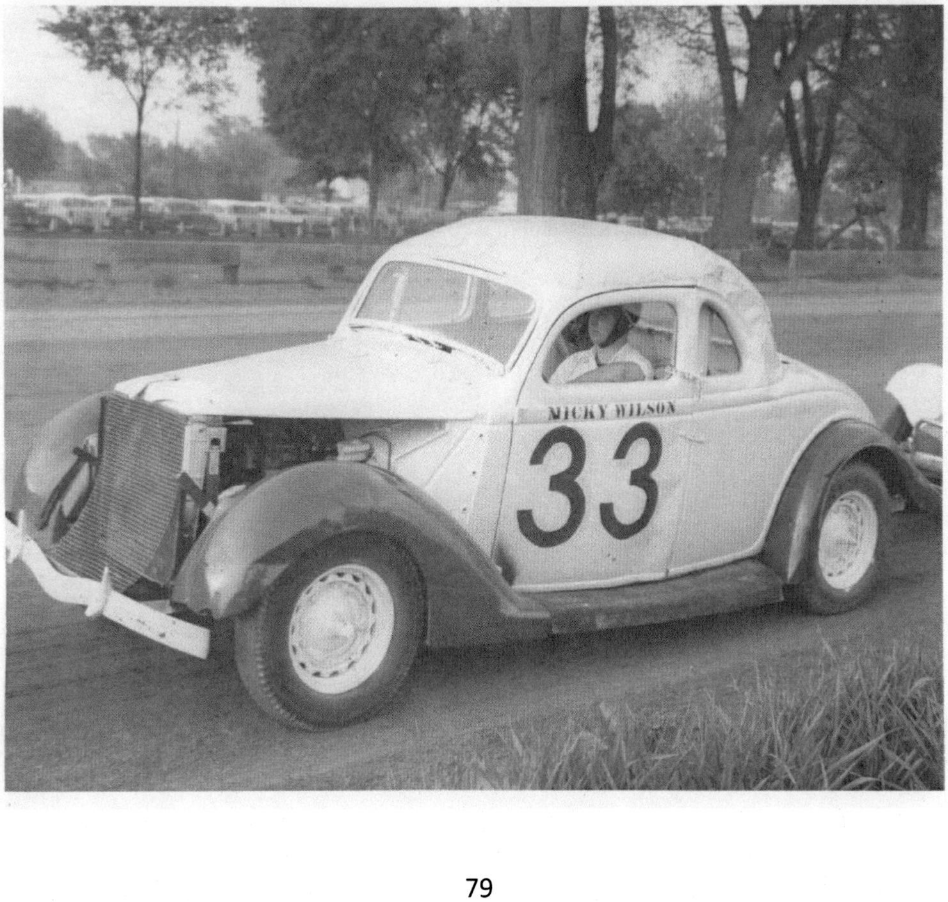
MICKY WILSON
33

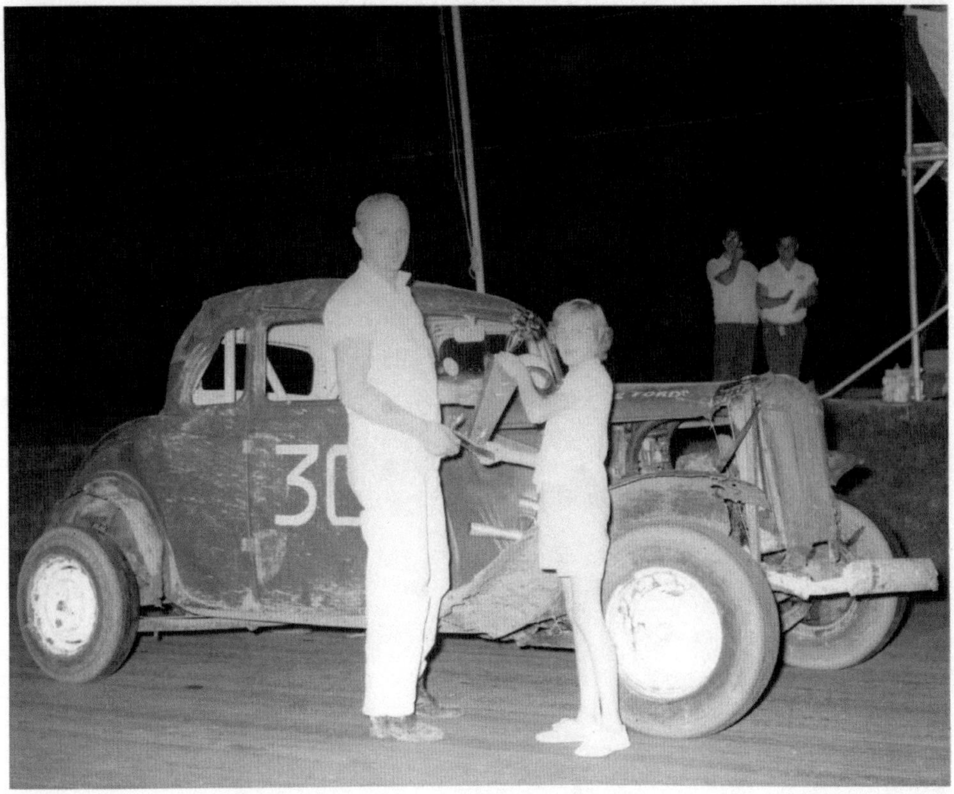

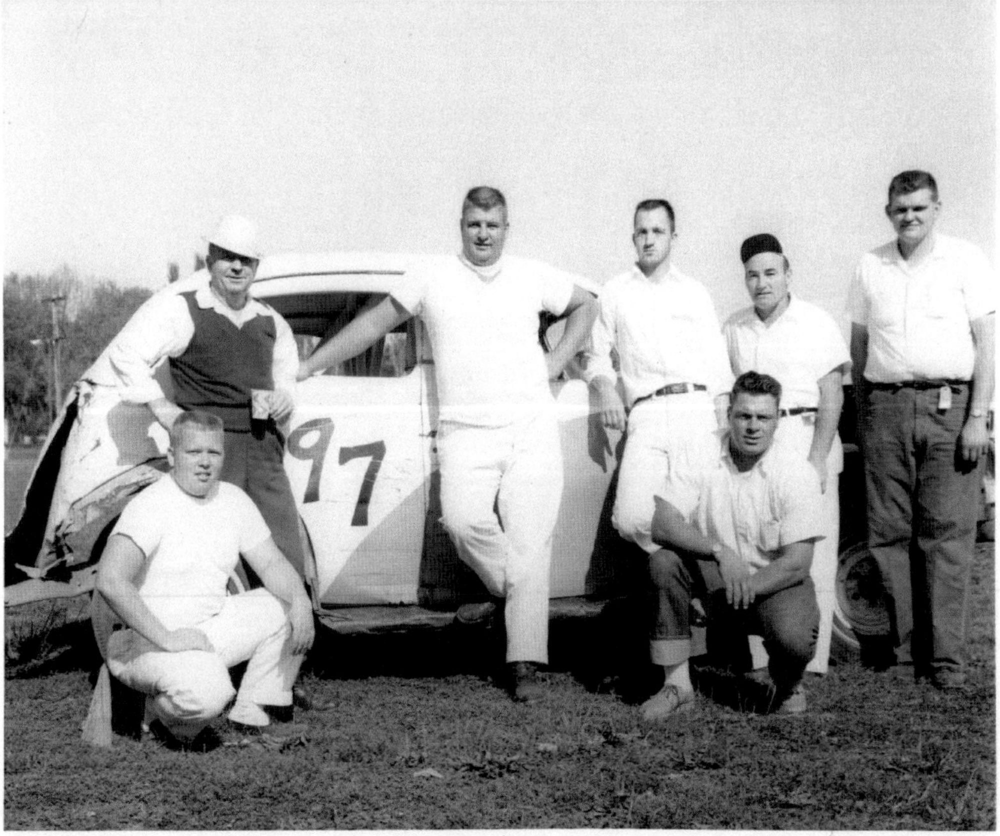
97

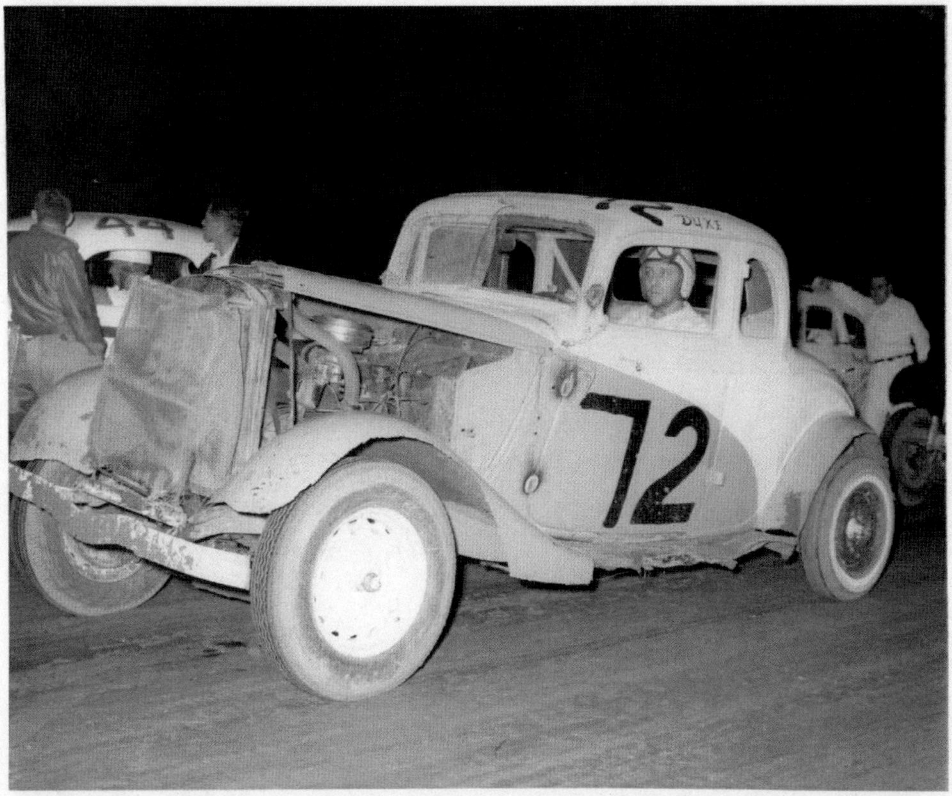
72

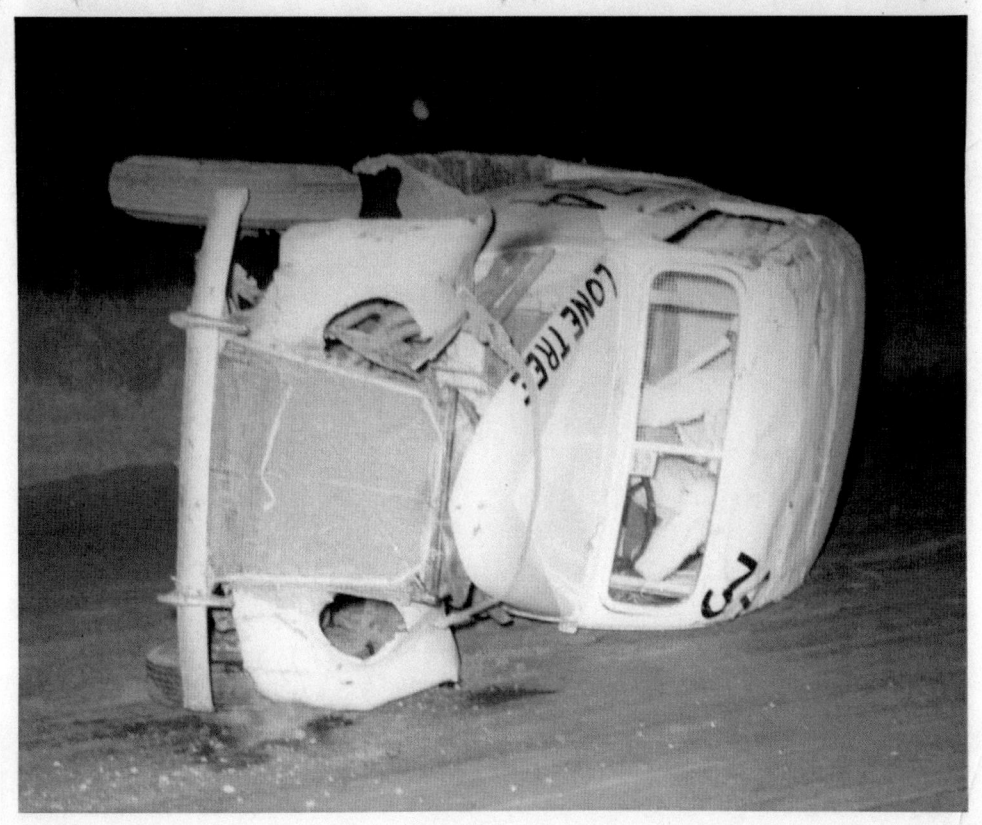

82

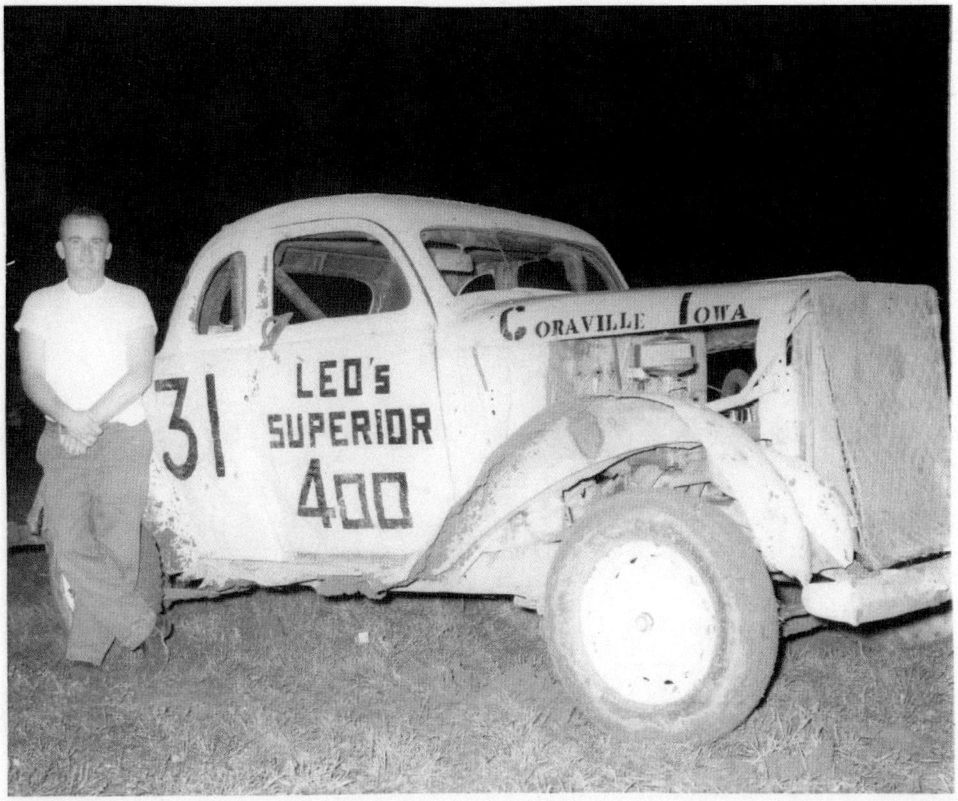
Coraville Iowa
31
LEO's
SUPERIOR
400

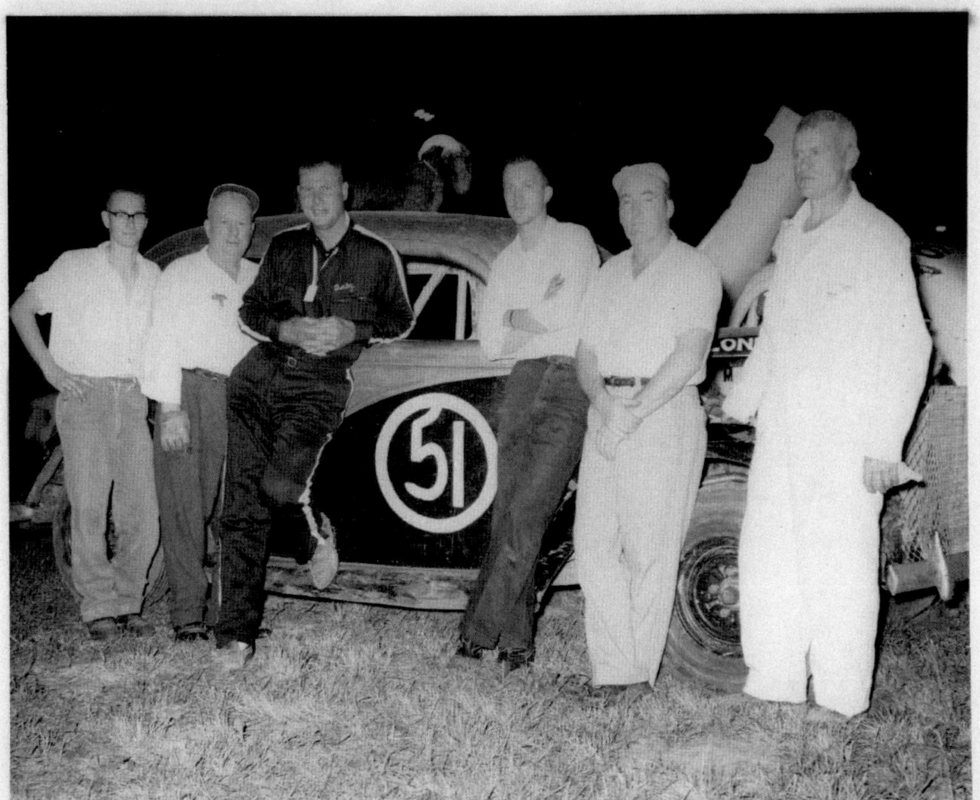
51

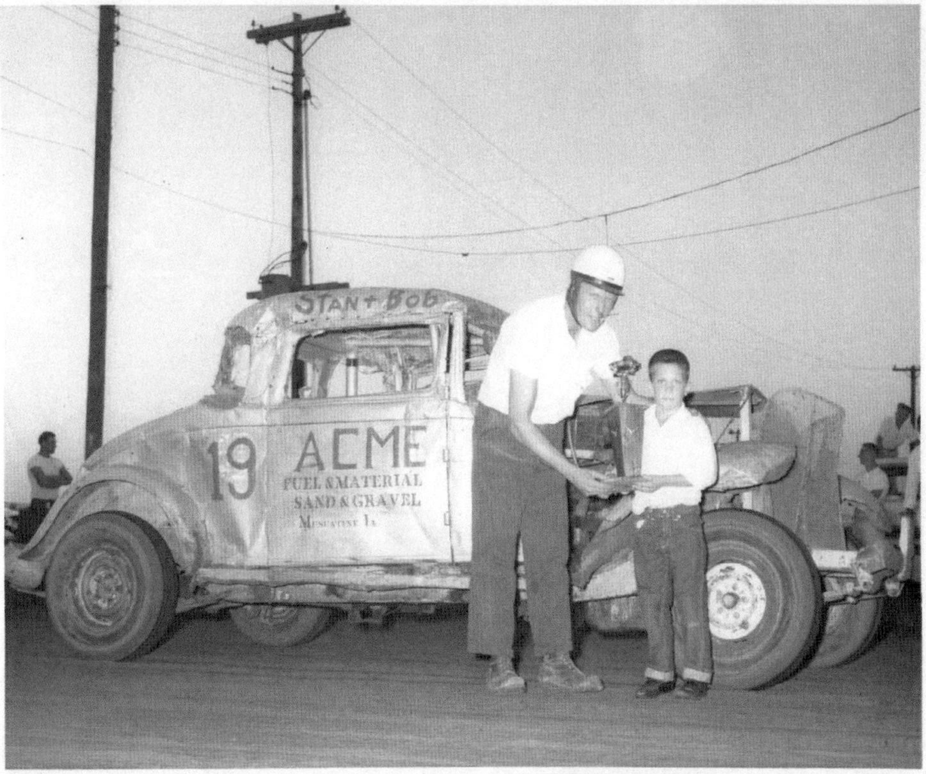
STAN + BOB
19
ACME
FUEL & MATERIAL
SAND & GRAVEL

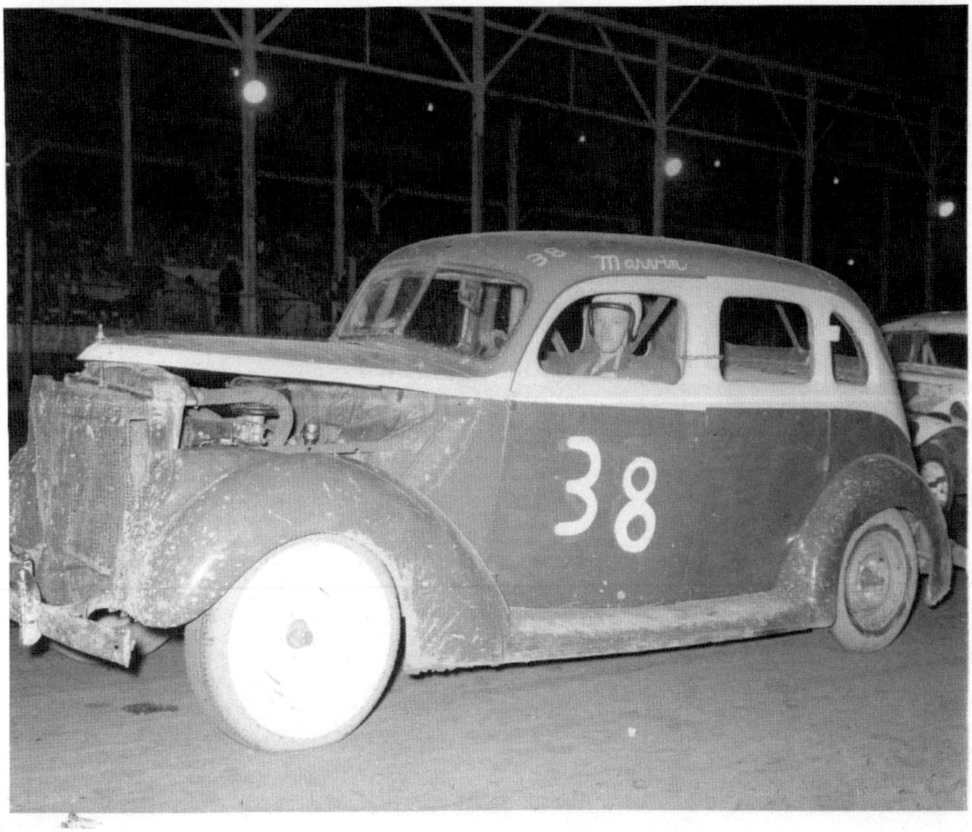
38 Marvin
38

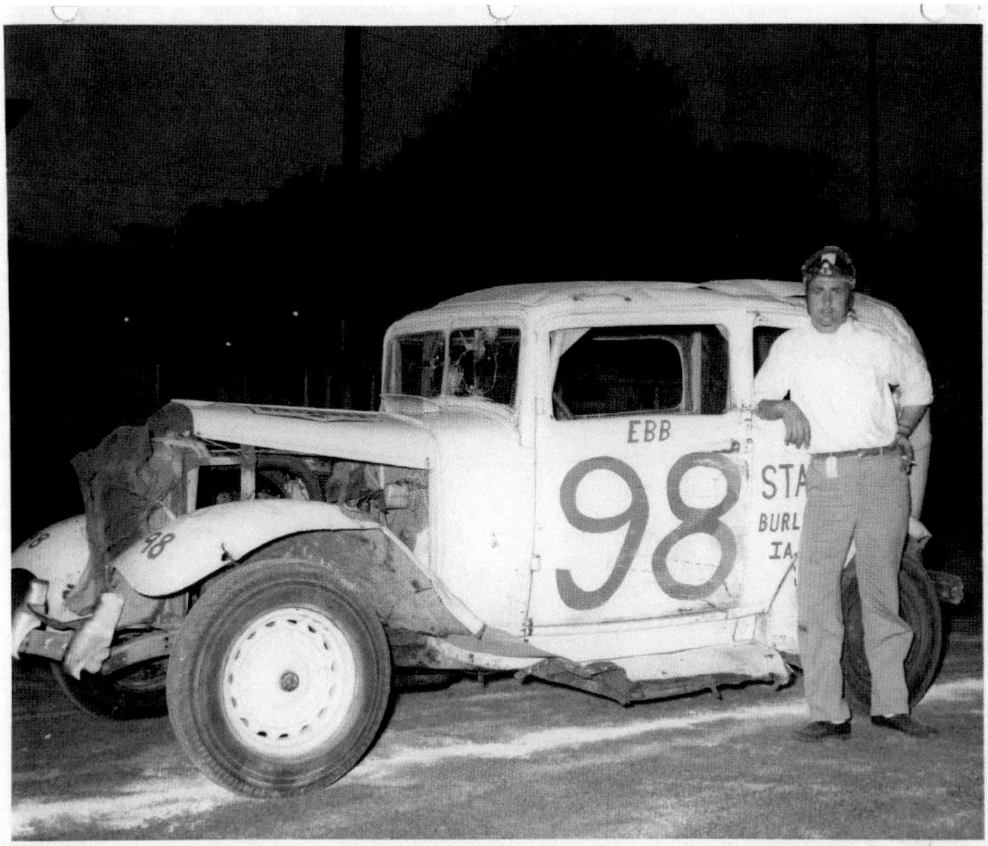
EBB
98

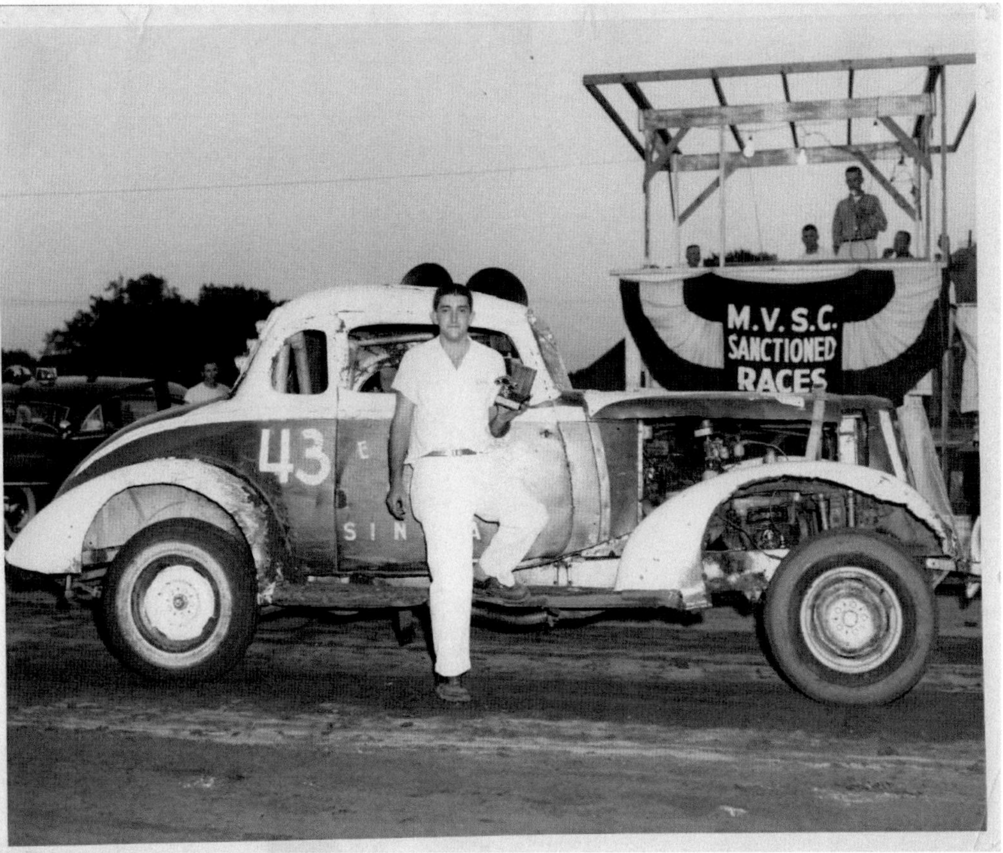
43
M.V.S.C.
SANCTIONED
RACES

86

87

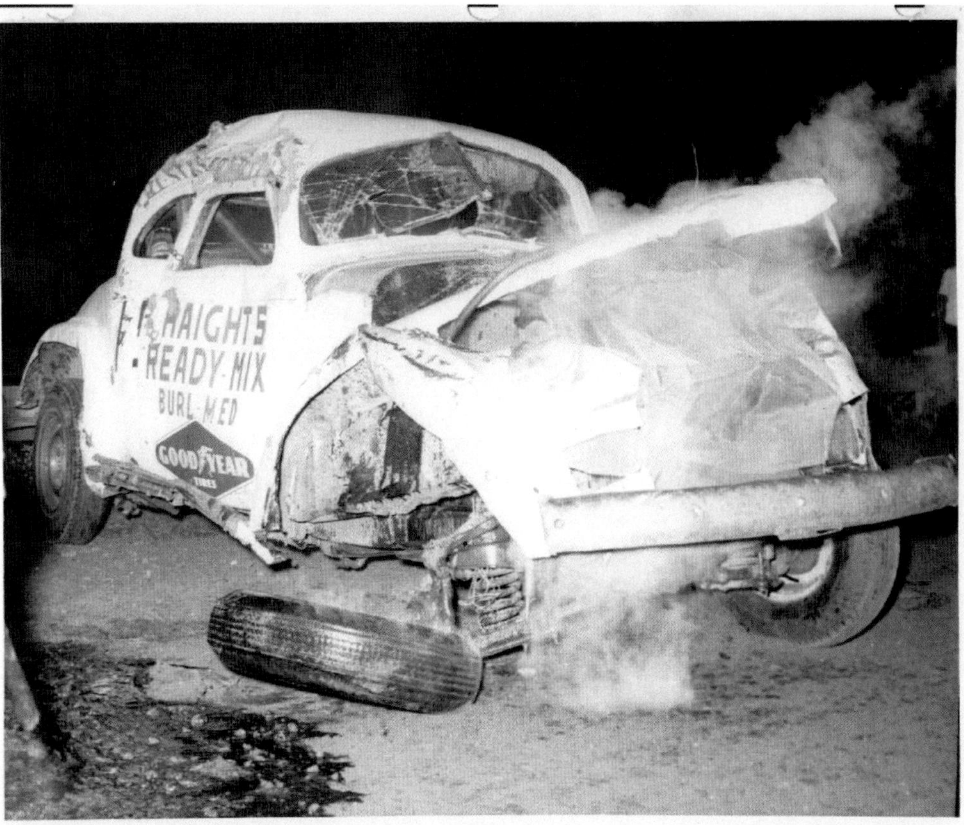
HAIGHTS
READY-MIX
BURL-MED
GOODYEAR

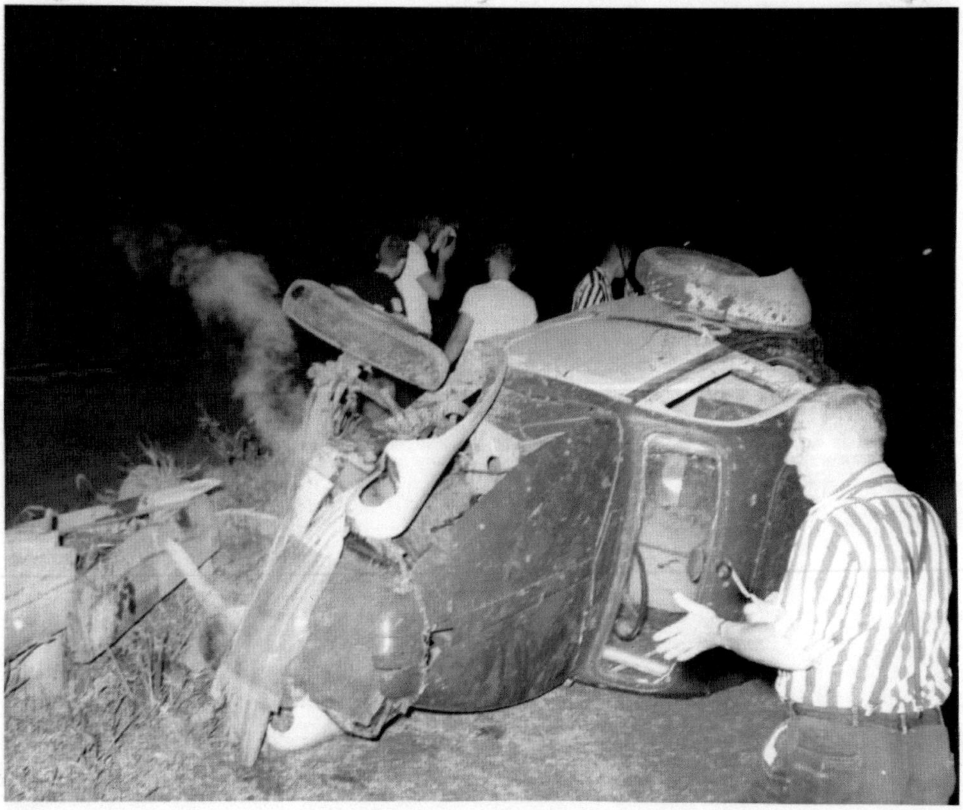

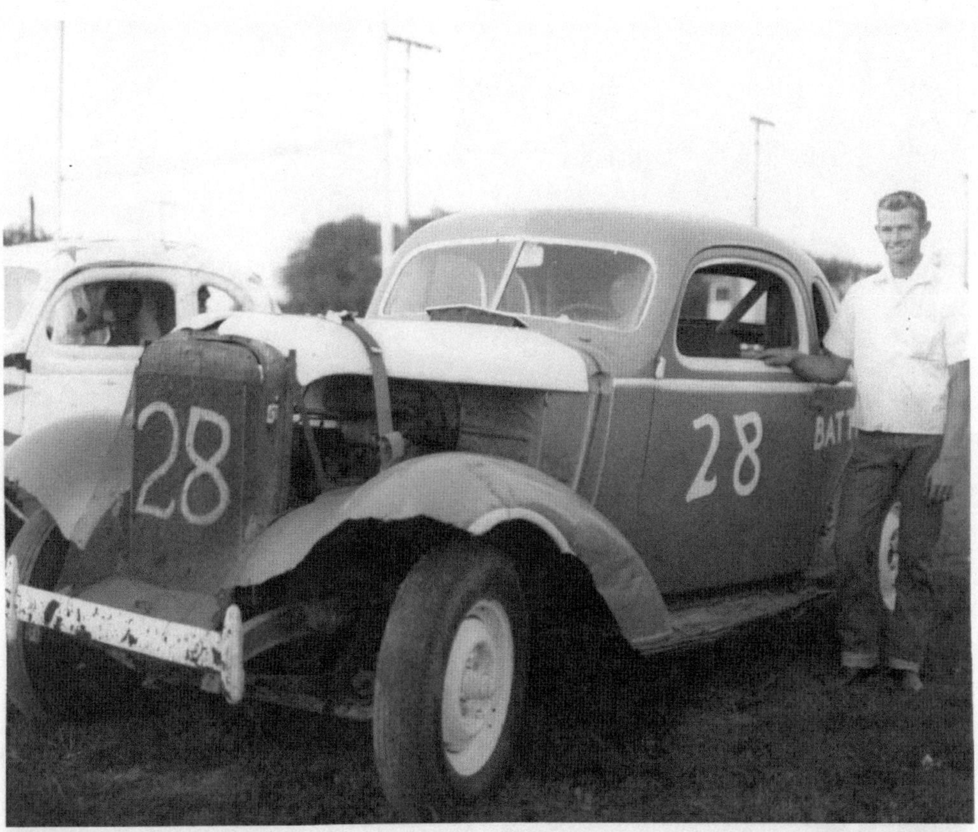
28
28

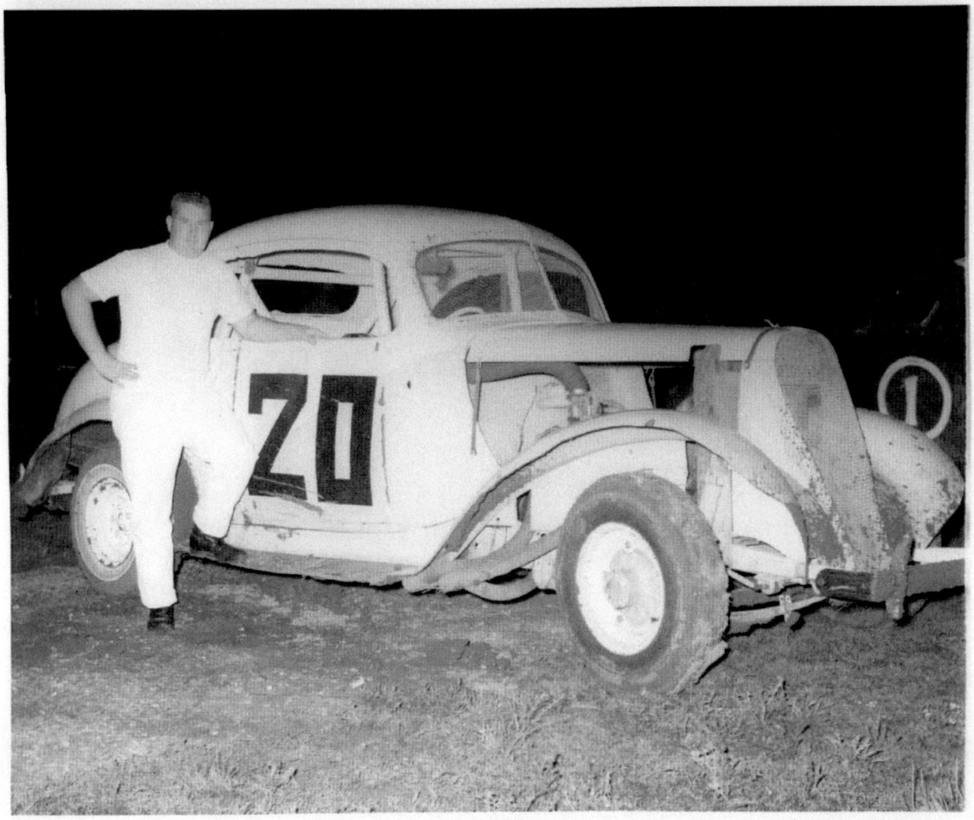
70
1

90

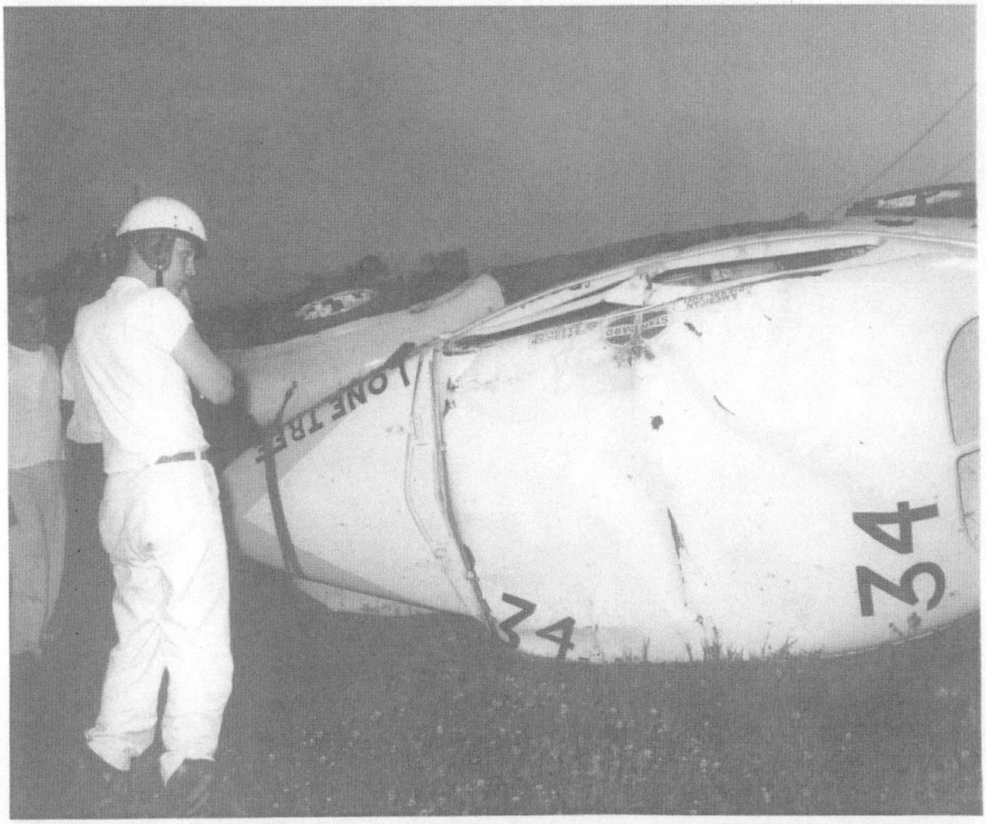
34
34

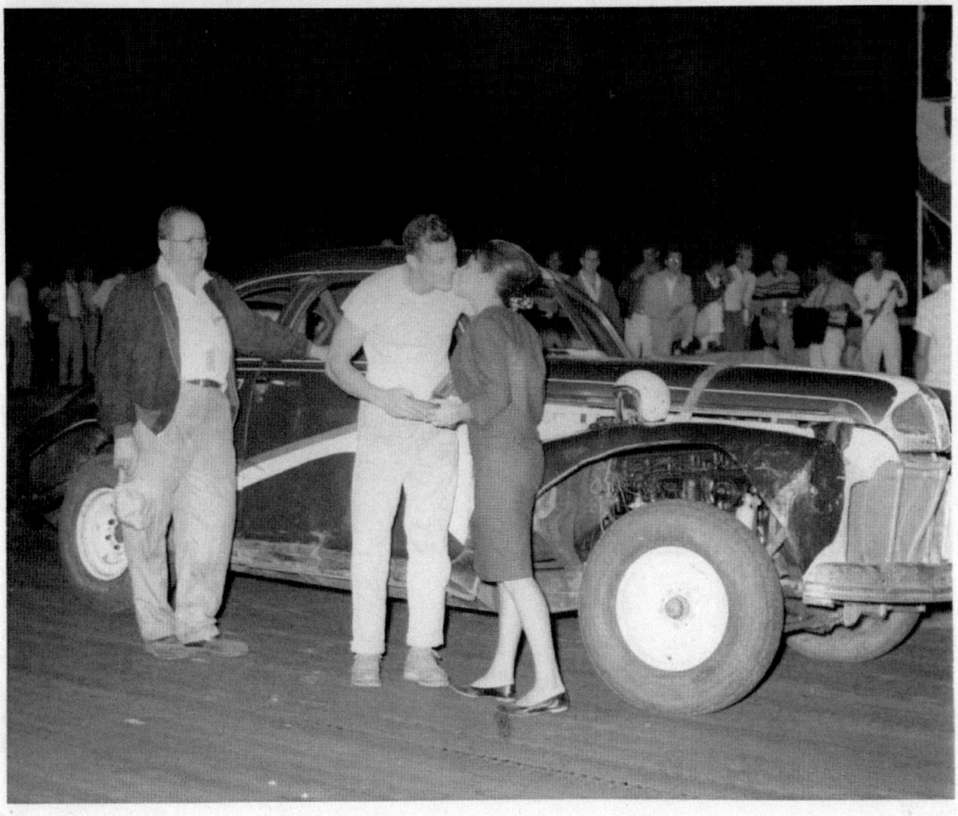

92

93

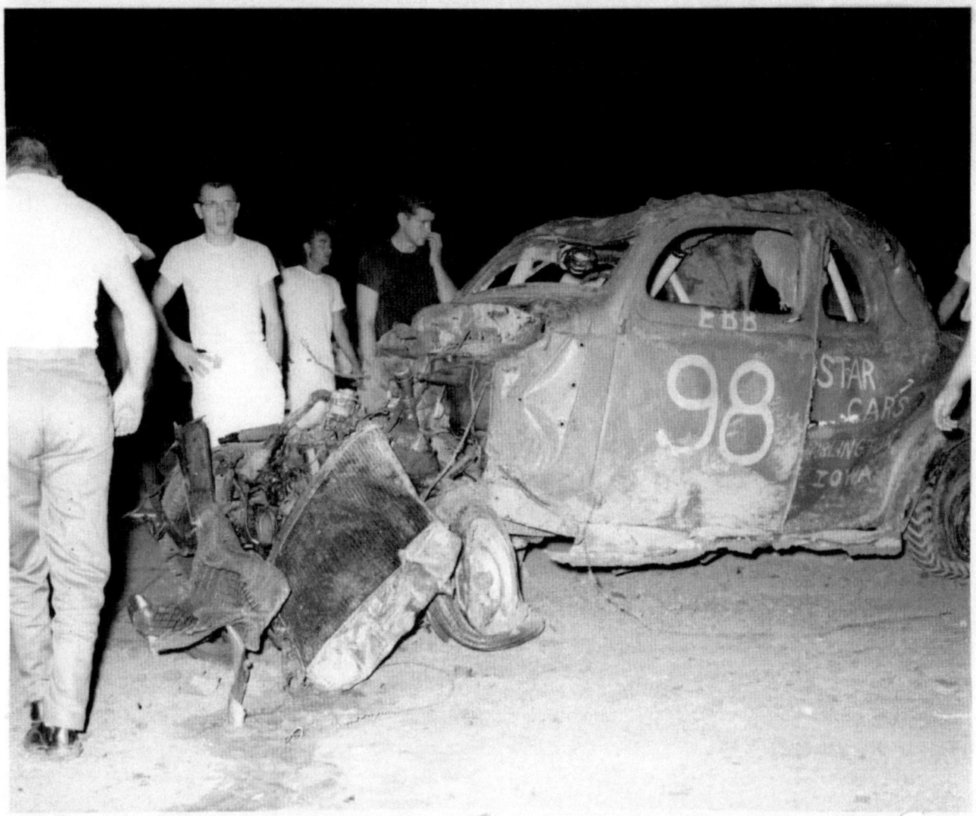
98
STAR
CARS
IOWA

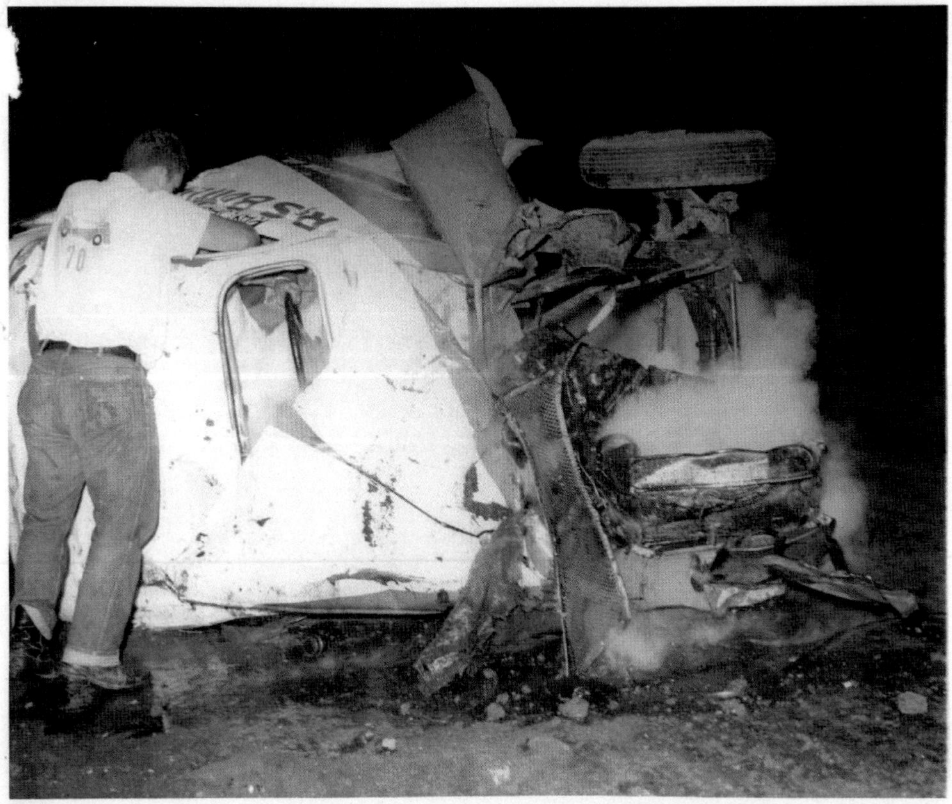
70

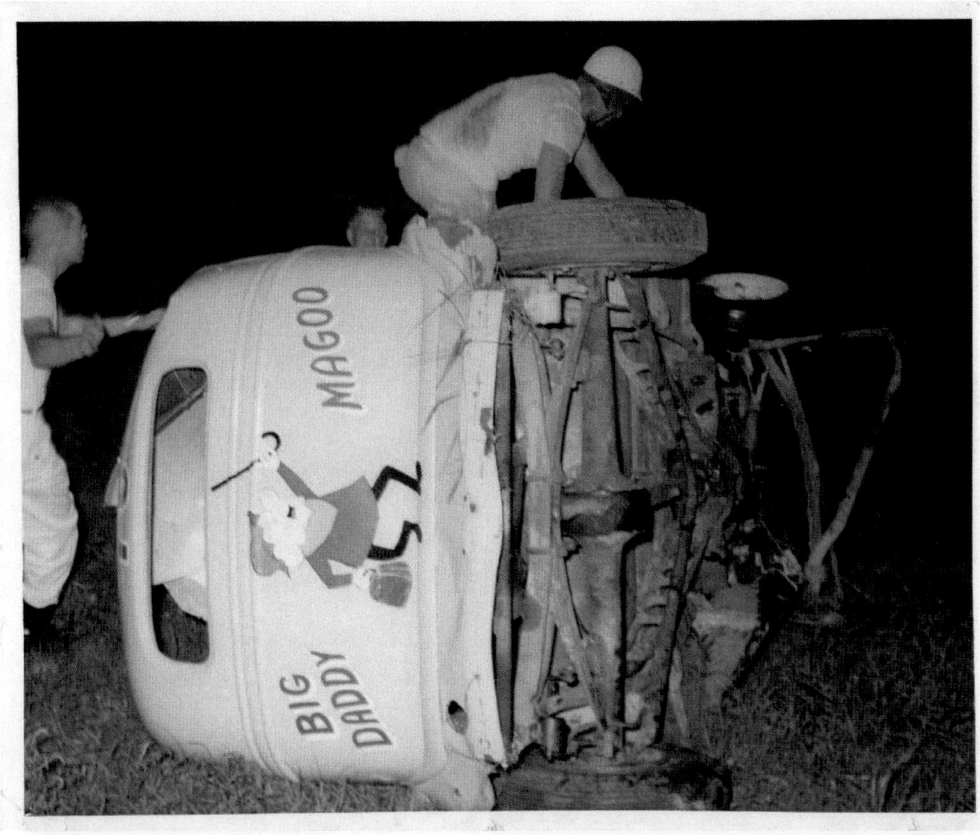
MAGOO
BIG
DADDY

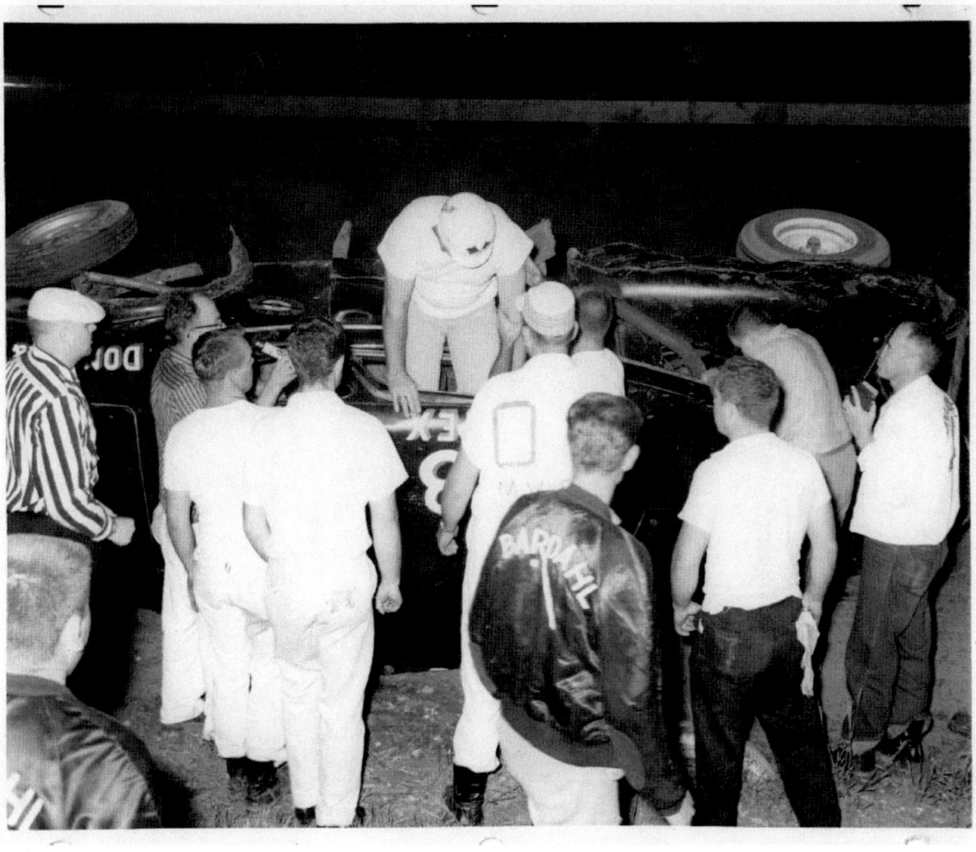
BARDAHL

96

97

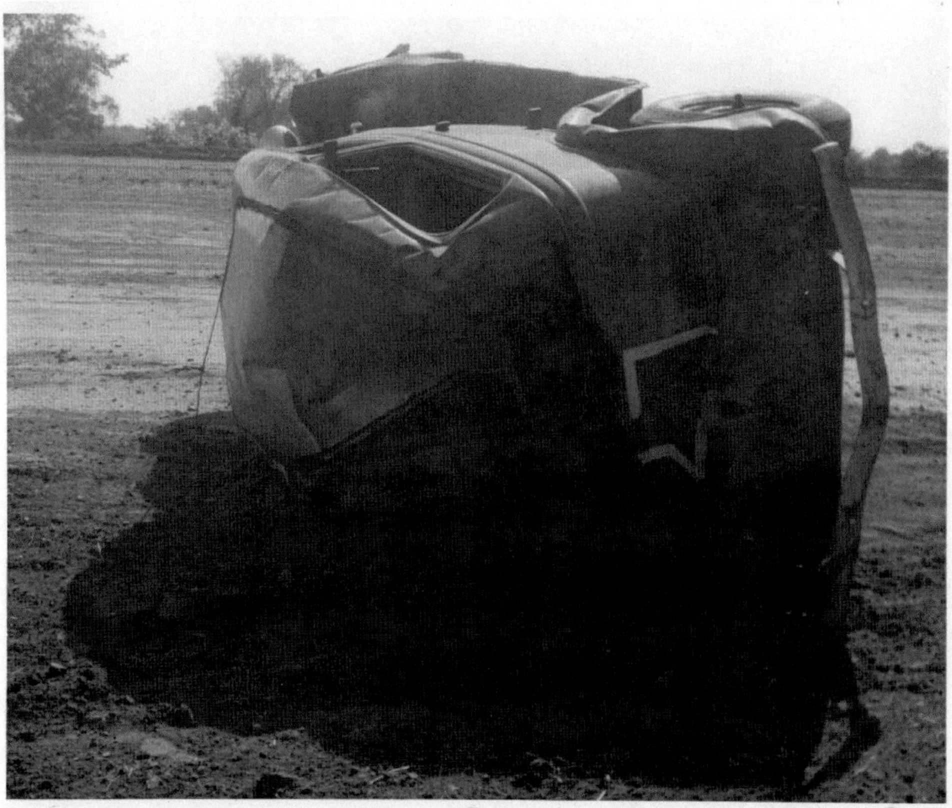

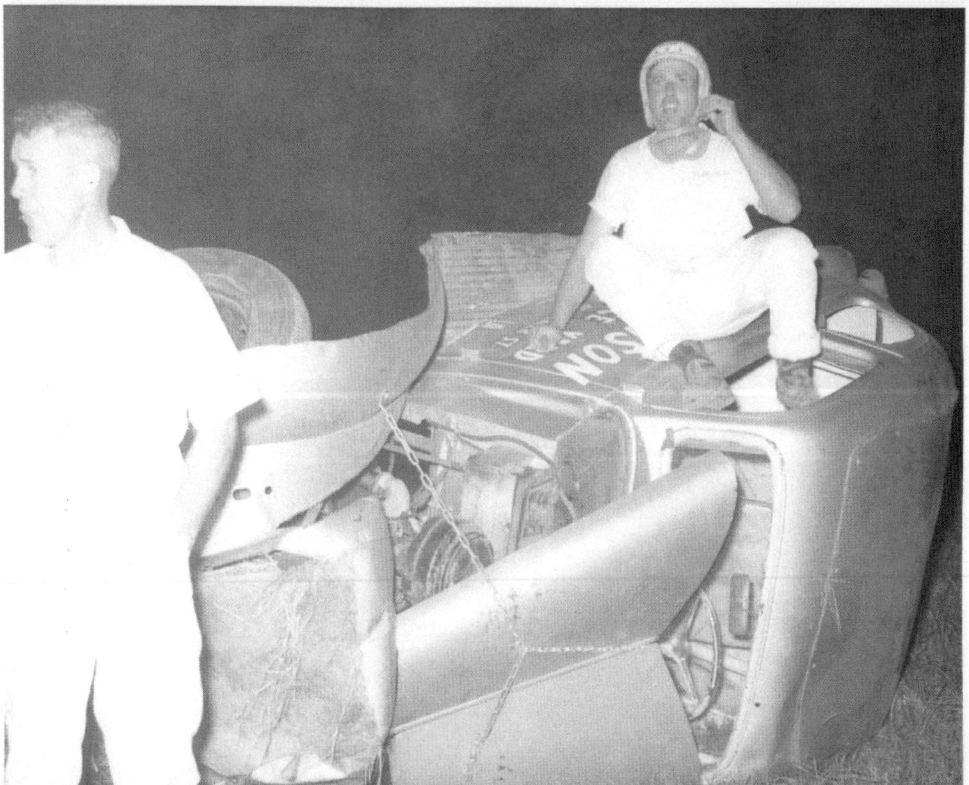

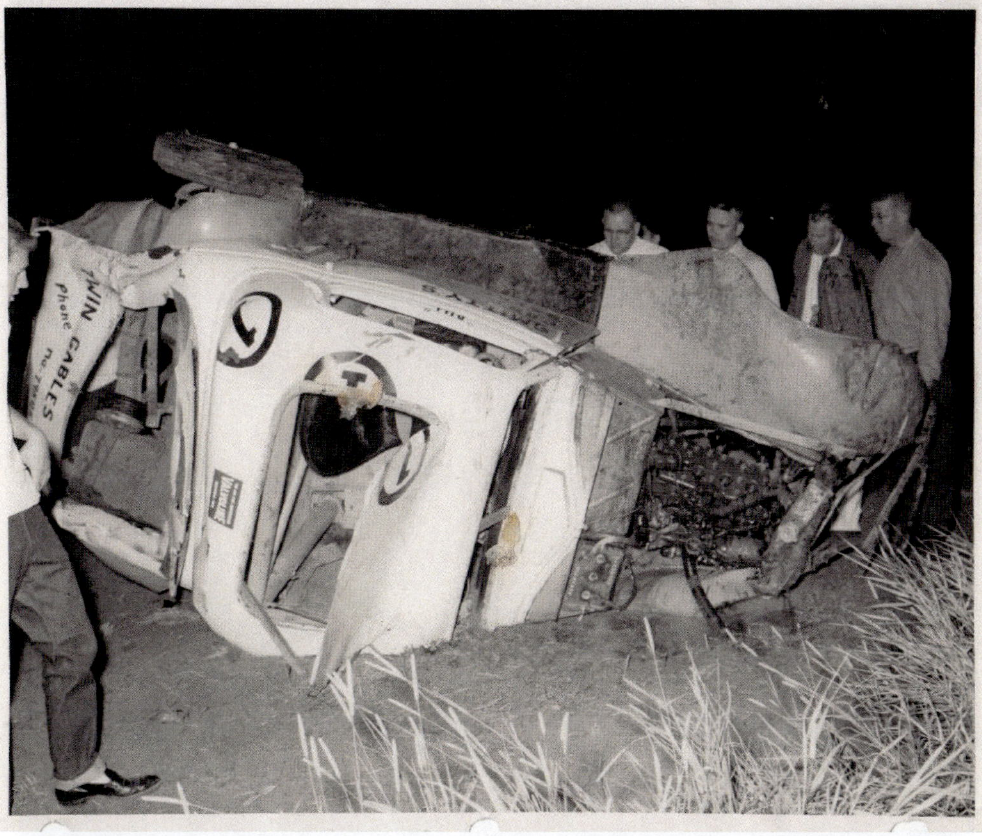
Phone CABLES

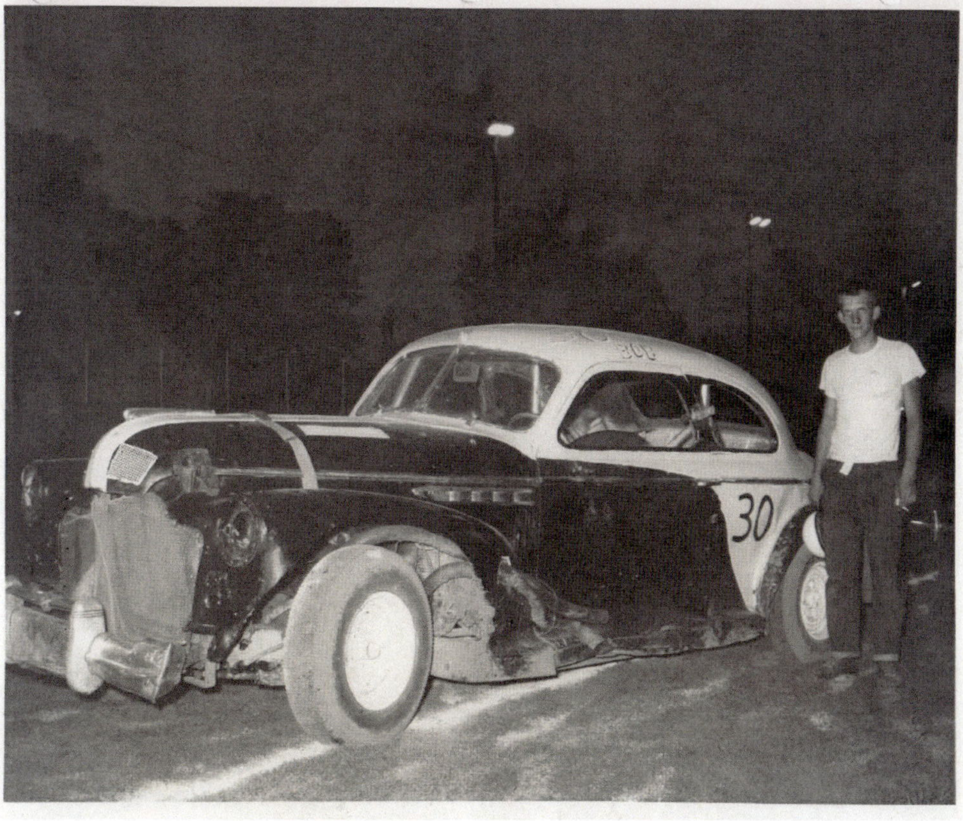
30

100

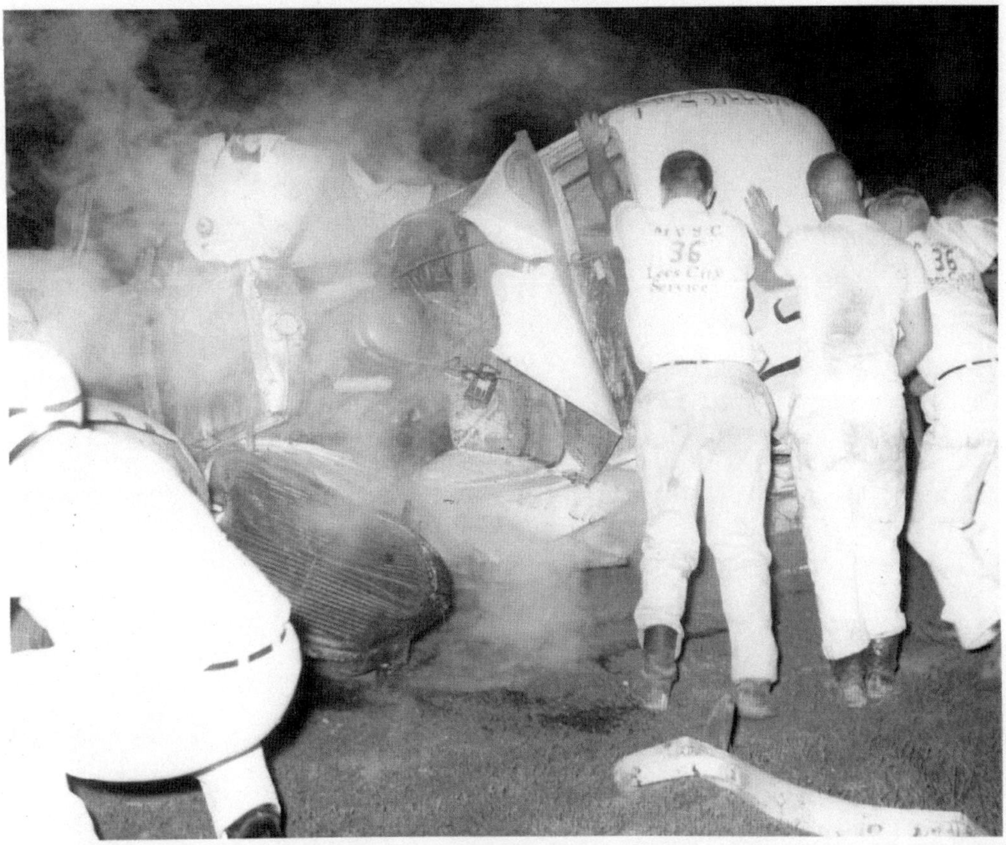
36

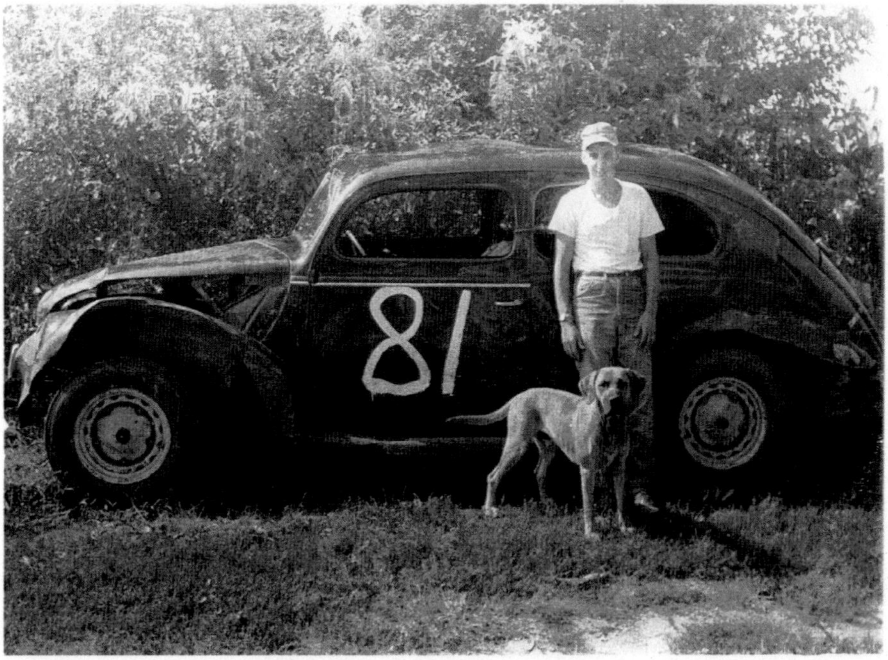
81

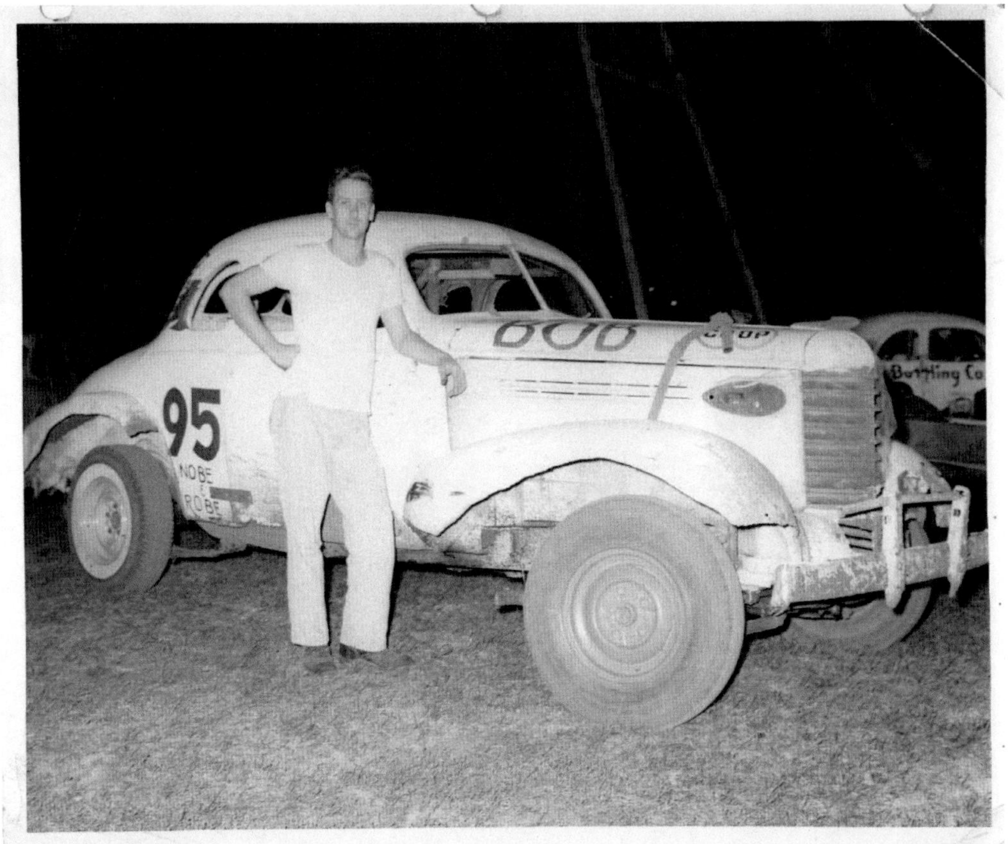
95

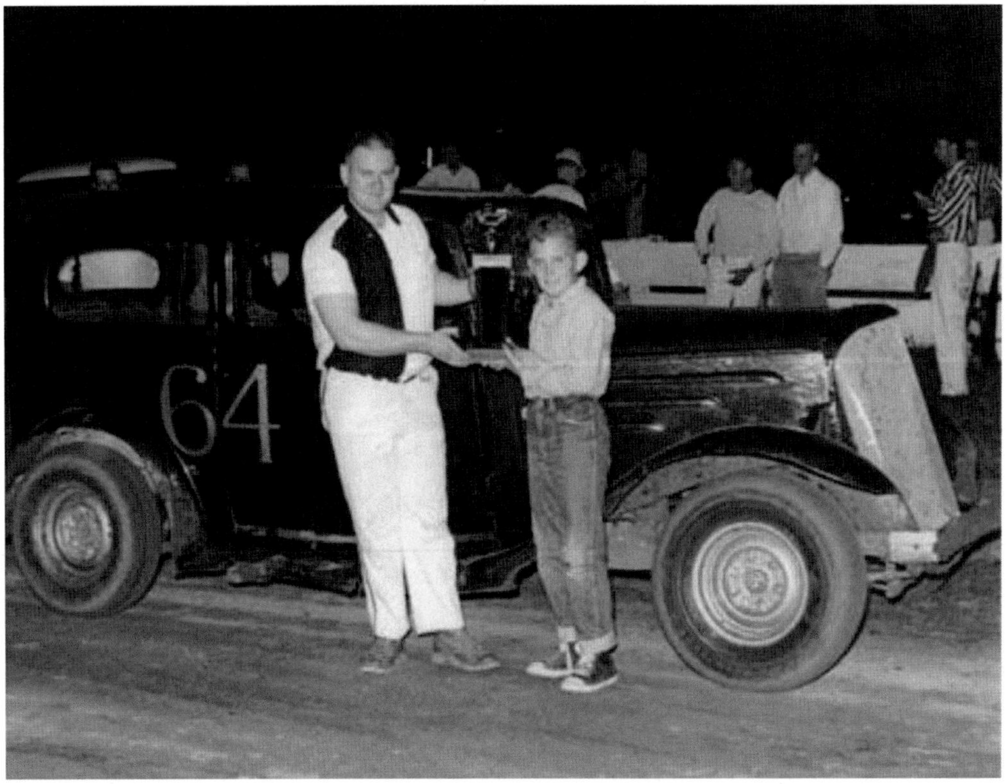
64

103

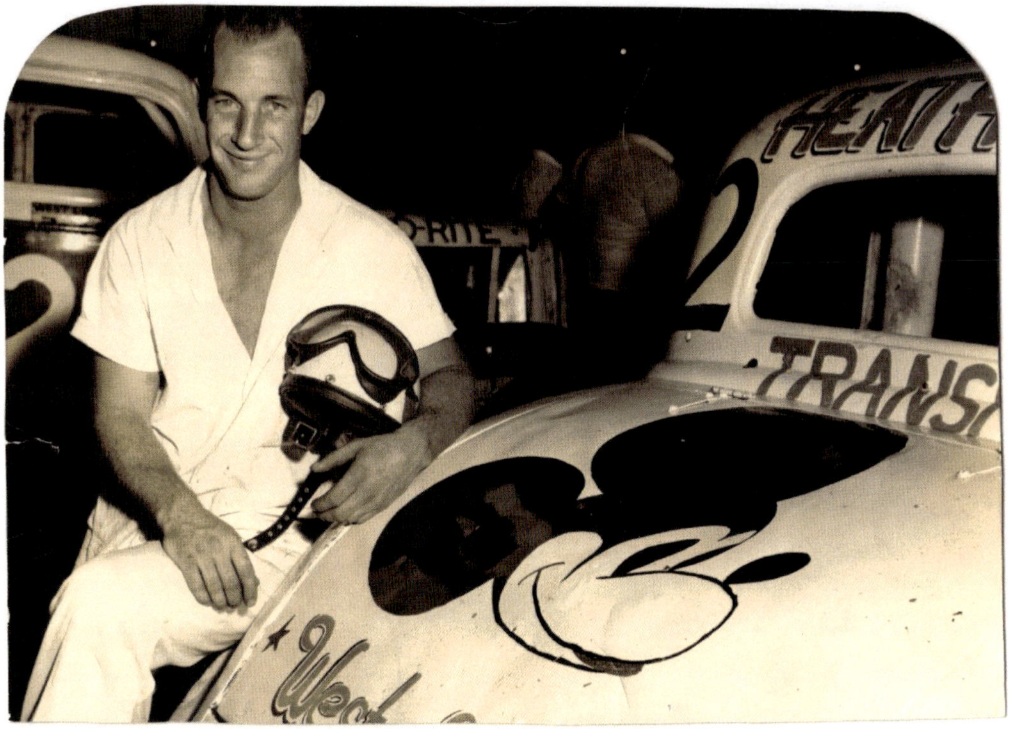

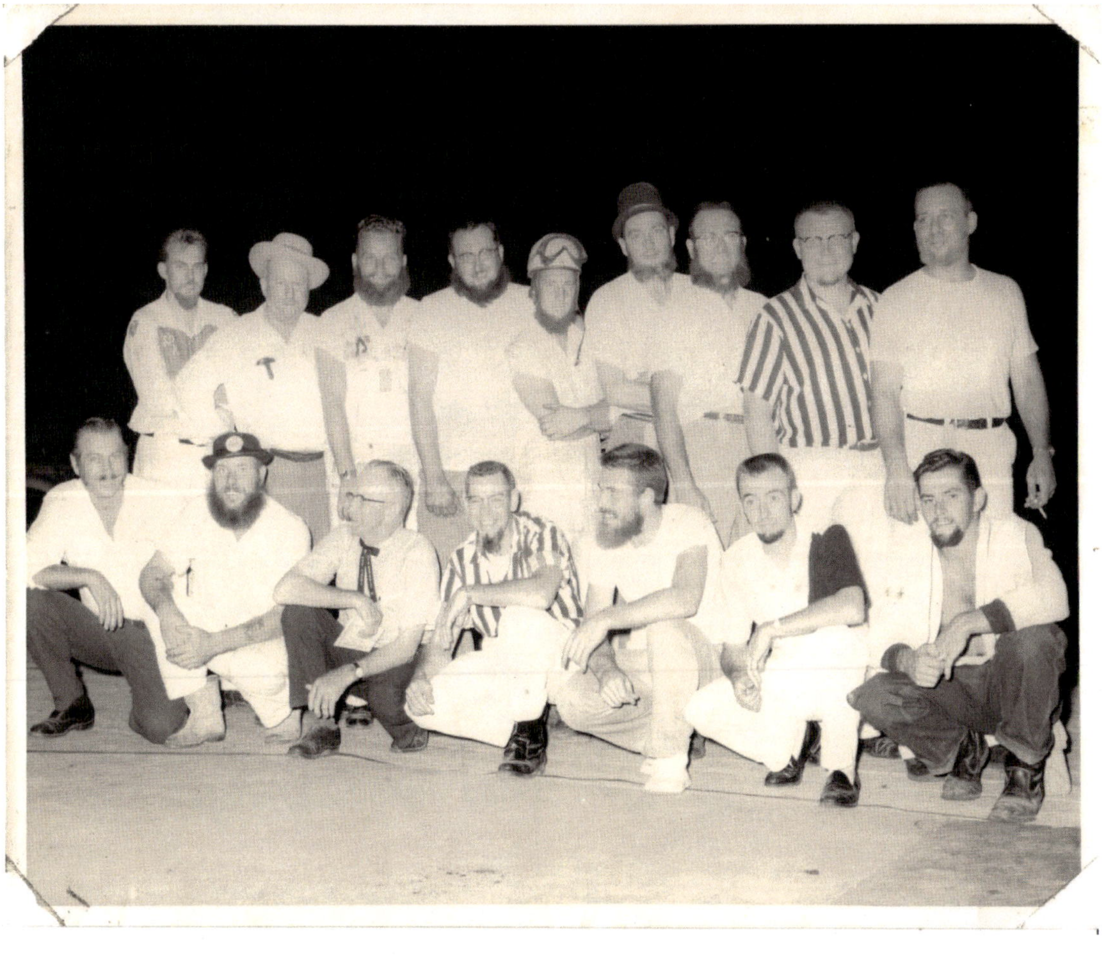

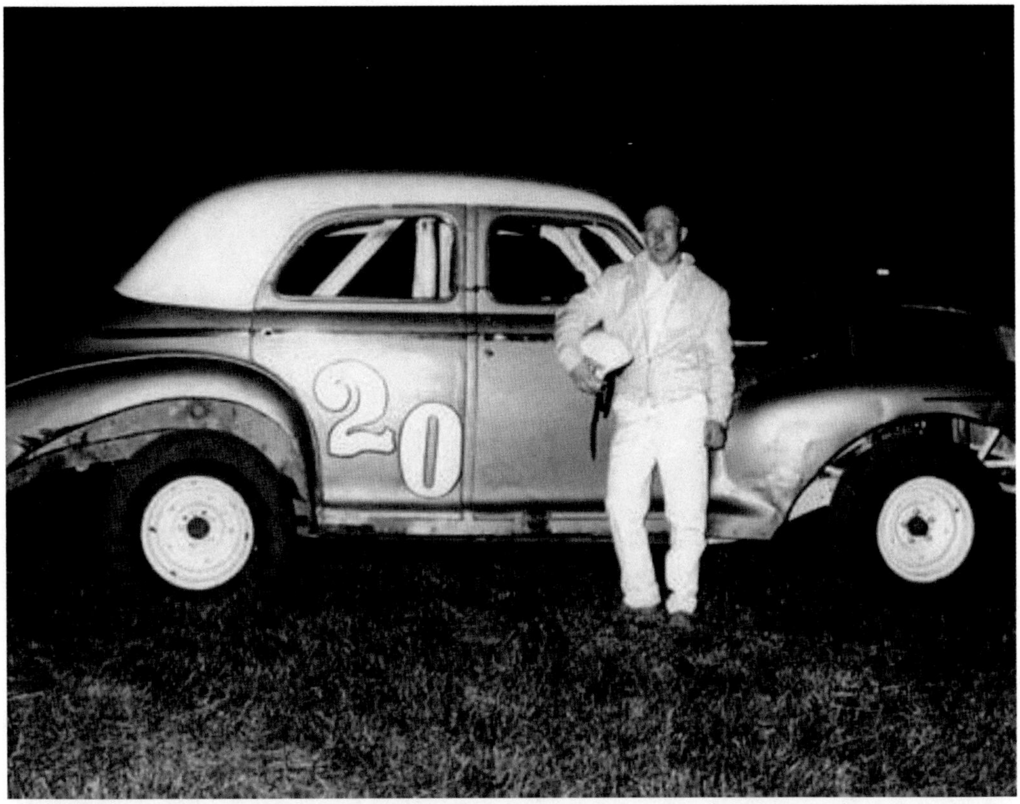
20

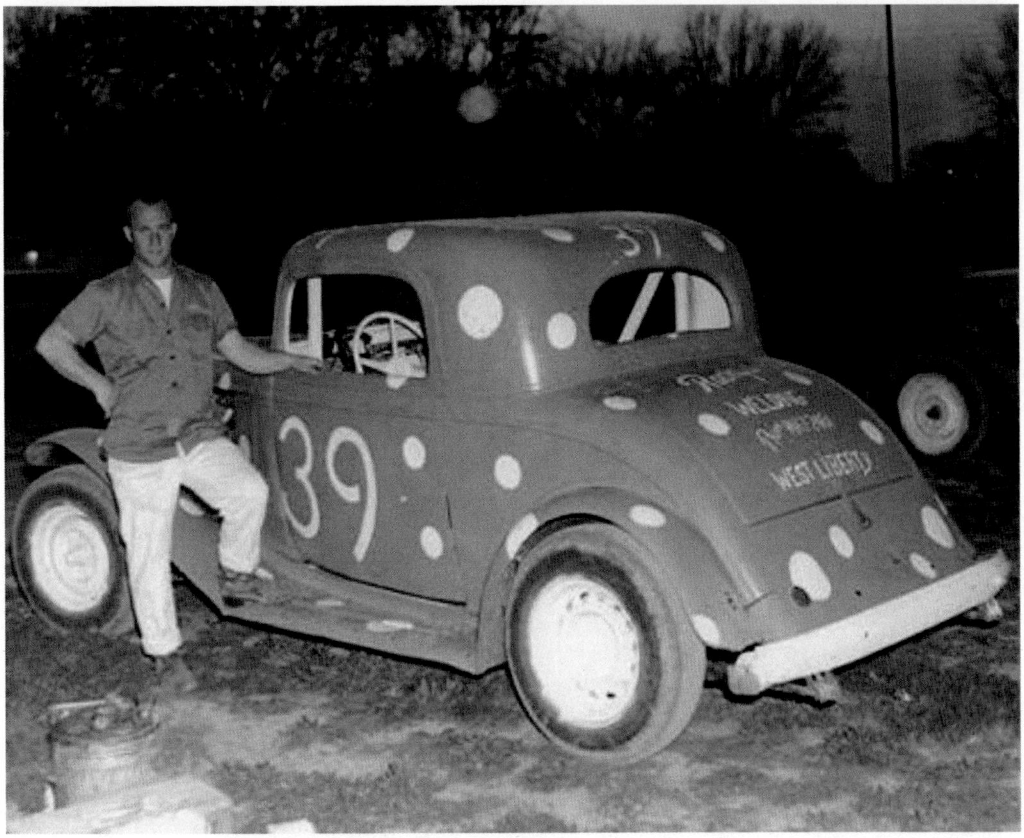
39
WELDING
WEST LIBERTY

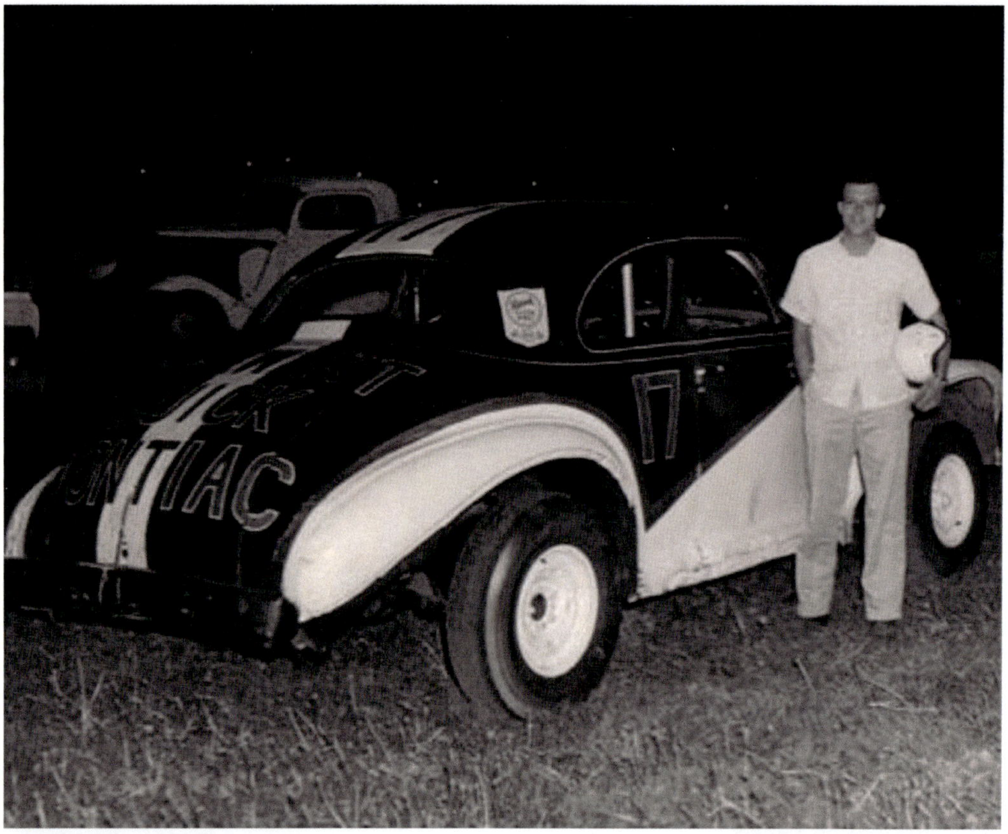
17

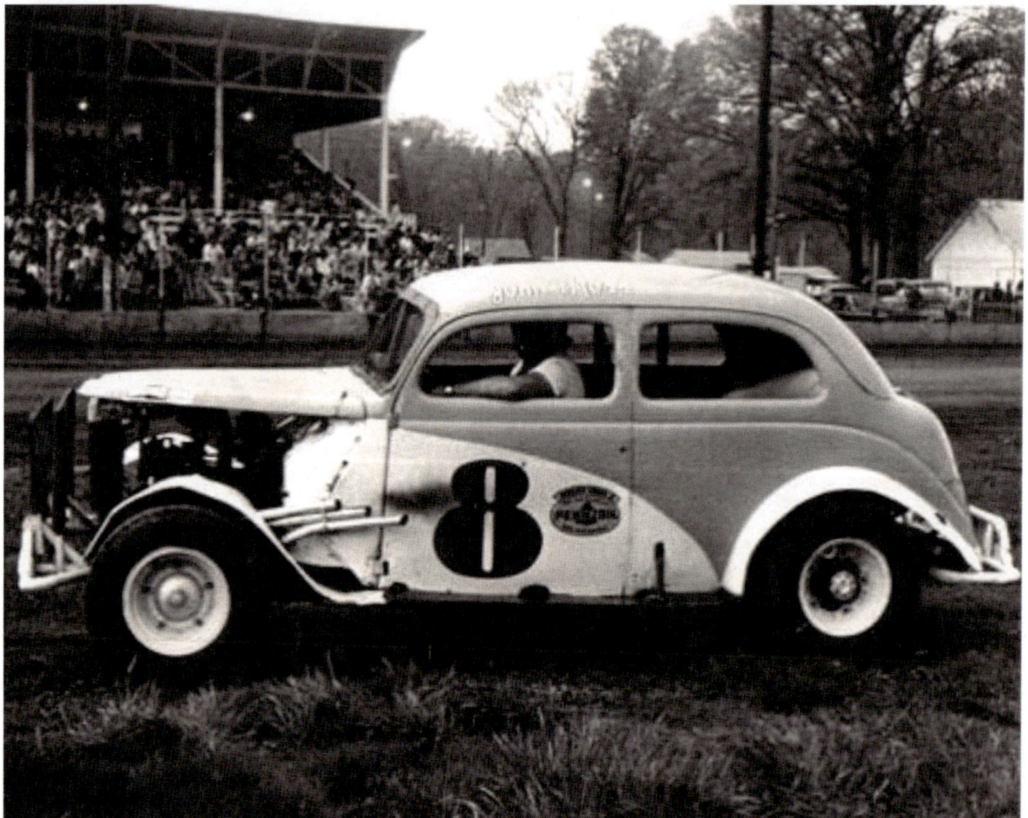
8